THE SAN PIPER

First published by O Books, 2008
O Books is an imprint of John Hunt Publishing Ltd., The Bothy, Deershot Lodge, Park Lane, Ropley, Hants, SO24 0BE, UK
office1@o-books.net
www.o-books.net

Distribution in:

UK and Europe
Orca Book Services
orders@orcabookservices.co.uk
Tel: 01202 665432 Fax: 01202 666219 Int. code (44)

USA and Canada
NBN
custserv@nbnbooks.com
Tel: 1 800 462 6420 Fax: 1 800 338 4550

Australia and New Zealand
Brumby Books
sales@brumbybooks.com.au
Tel: 61 3 9761 5535 Fax: 61 3 9761 7095

Far East (offices in Singapore, Thailand, Hong Kong, Taiwan)
Pansing Distribution Pte Ltd
kemal@pansing.com
Tel: 65 6319 9939 Fax: 65 6462 5761

South Africa
Alternative Books
altbook@peterhyde.co.za
Tel: 021 447 5300 Fax: 021 447 1430

Design: Stuart Davies

ISBN: 978 1 84694 092 7

A CIP catalogue record for this book is available from the British Library.

Printed in the US by Maple Vail

THE SAN PIPER

UYS LAFRA

Winchester, UK
Washington, USA

CONTENTS

This Book is for my Wife
Tilla

PREFACE

Staring at the remains of a once proud and nimble springbok, I thought aloud:

"Yes, life **is** a bitch – and then you die..."

The Bushman replied: "Ace, that's quite a statement considering what you wrote about."

My mind elsewhere, I didn't consciously hear him but without expecting an answer, he continued: "You've expressed your opinion with similar phrases over the past few days; do you really mean that, or is it just a way to escape your frustration with life?"

After a while I realized that he had asked me something to which any response might have laid bare the essence of my deepest self, the makeup of my own soul. I found no answer and neither could I think of anything appropriate to say. Frustration drew its net of confusion closer and closer: I knew that my comment was provoked by nothing but ignorance.

******

Believe me, it took a lot of courage and discarding of personal convictions to write this book. After meeting an extraordinary Bushman and his friend in the Kalahari and spending several days with them, I knew that there was no getting away from it. Teecha's personality and spirit forced me to sit down and write.

Until today I wonder if fate had something to do with our acquaintance or something much deeper. It was probably the latter, for I sincerely hope to meet him again, although I know now that it could only happen in another place and in another time.

Throughout history, man's lack of understanding the fundamental principles of life has always been a factor which has led to some ridiculous assumptions and beliefs.

As the real truths and laws under which life and the universe operate were gradually uncovered, so man slowly had to change his mind. Yet his newly found knowledge caused more and more complications, so that new assumptions had to be made and new theories dreamt up. The process seems to continue in never-ending circles.

We live in a fantastic age of discovery and new knowledge is gained exponentially in all spheres of life. Unfortunately we cannot adjust fast enough. We cling to our comfort zones, acting like primitive beings full of superstitious rubbish, and persist in waging wars against each other, and then we fear the Armageddon, not realizing that it will only be caused by our own ignorance and stupidity.

What the Bushman had told me and what this book is about, is that we should view facts and beliefs from different angles – after which we may just be able to fit a few more pieces into the puzzle of existence and into the purpose of life. We have many super-senses and powers that we do not know about, do not understand or do not want to use. Into my own life comes a supposed-to-be savage and illiterate Bushman showing me how we should put those powers to work, how to enrich our lives and how to gain spiritual, material and financial fulfillment. All of those senses and powers are easy to master and could significantly change our lives and our outlook on life for the better, unless used negatively, as I had learned.

I sincerely hope that all of us will get a bit more out of this life than merely existing. To experience happiness and to live our lives to the full, this time around, is what life's all about.

In all modesty and with a remarkable old man's inspiration, I hope that this book will answer some of the questions we all have. With that, and like he did to mine, Teecha will probably not leave his short acquaintance with your mind for some time to come.

Uys Lavra

Only when we pause to wonder
do we go beyond the limits
of our **incredible** minds

Why are we so worried about the future
when we already know what it holds for us?

Man is allowed to create his own future and
for that reason he is given great powers.

To follow any dream there are many roads to
choose from and many means to achieve it.
Reason, amongst others, is a powerful tool,
but before any decision is made the knowledge
of what direction to take is already there.

If man doesn't use his powers or listen to them,
he may quickly lose his way;
Intuition, for instance,

Is his gift of knowing things in advance...

*****

4

THE ENCOUNTER

The Landcruiser churns through the thick sand of the Kalahari dunes. In low range and four-wheel drive engaged, I hardly manage to keep it going in third gear for more than 50 meters. Changing into second I wonder if I'm still on the right road. To tell the truth, I lost it four times this morning and had to backtrack. Losing half an hour every time was enough to dampen whatever enthusiasm I had for this journey. Apart from that, it wasted precious fuel and the gauge was nearing empty. Back to third gear.

An old saying in this part of the world goes: 'When in doubt, take the most used trail'. This easily fools you, as the most used one is often a dead end, forcing travelers to go back to where they took the wrong turn in the first place. Because of this the wrong trail appears to be more used and a map is of little use – that goes for a GPS too. I passed the last rusty and illegible signpost near Mamuno at the border between Namibia and Botswana. There, a day and a half ago, I left all traces of civilization and drove south...

"OK Uys, now drop the revs slightly... take it easy... and whatever you do, don't stop."

In front of me the track doesn't look much different from the last 100 kilometers, but the color of the sand has changed.

"Steady speed... keep it there..."

The Landcruiser starts rocking like a boat, engine whining and wheels spinning up sand and dust. Swaying left and right as the front wheels follow the deep tracks by themselves, the vehicle bounces, jumps, hops, creaks under the strain and rolls back and forth all at the same time – enough to make anyone seasick.

"After this one, I must check if everything is still tied down... and take another compass bearing."

WHAM!

Instinctively I floor the accelerator pedal as the left front wheel hits the hole. The wheel barely makes it out but the sand gives way. In a split second, I realize the inevitable. "Too late, you idiot – why don't you look where you're going?" but as a last resort: "Steer left... No!" It was another mistake. WHAM! once more and "Dammit!" as my head bumps the roof. "Keep the front wheels straight!"

It's survival mode now and I floor the accelerator. "Ouch!" The steering wheel spins clockwise and knocks my knuckles painfully. Grabbing it firmly, I try to force the wheels straight. They don't budge and the engine stalls.

"Damn, ant bear!"

Closing the windows and vents to stop choking in dust, I scoff at myself with disdain: "You stupid fool!"

The speedometer reading shows that it took me eight hours to do no more than 70 miles or 100 kilometers.

A taunting voice on my shoulder says: "Excellent, Uys, exactly what you expected. You knew that only one vehicle on this route was taking a silly chance and worse so, for doing it alone."

"So what," I console myself, "I'm just solidly bogged down in the middle of nowhere – it's not that bad – and it's lunchtime, so I would have had to stop anyway."

Stepping out, I think about playing my little 'glad' game but decide against it. With scrambled thoughts I untie a fold-up chair from the roof-carrier and start to carry it to the shade of a large umbrella thorn tree, about 20 meters from the road. The vehicle stands at an odd angle, with the left rear wheel well and truly stuck in the ant bear hole. These pig-like nocturnal animals are fairly common but shy. Weighing about 65 kilograms, 140 pounds, they like digging rather large and deep holes and often, just to be spiteful, in roads.

"To hell with it and I hope the damn ant bear gets a pain…" On second thoughts: "Calm down Uys, you'd better inspect the damage."

I turn back to the vehicle and summing up the problem makes me reach for a cold beer, saying sarcastically: "I'm glad the fridge still works... and I'm glad its not another flat tire."

Taking the chair, I walk to the tree and sit down in its shade. Mentally and physically I'm hot but the beer is cold. I roll the cool can across my cheeks, forehead and chest. "Thank goodness for technology... and for heavens' sake, what on earth caused me to take this road?"

The silence is audible as only the silence of the Kalahari can be. Not a blade of grass moves. There isn't a bird chirping nor an animal in sight. Not a sound.

"This must be the meaning of silence," I decide. Opening the beer can sounds like a pistol shot and half the contents fizz out. I gulp down as much of the froth as possible. For a minute or two I try to figure out why I'm here but no reason comes to mind. Shimmering heat waves distort the horizon, like phantoms on the edge of a great lake.

More sand gives way under the vehicle and it slips deeper into the hole. The sound startles me back to reality.

At the same time the Kalahari sun beetles or cicadas start up. They are little insects hiding in shrubs and trees and living off the sap from young stems. Males have a drum-like sound organ underneath their bodies which they use to try to attract female company by producing a screeching, whining sound, which rings through your ears as a monotonous tone. Thousands of them all start screeching at once, as if an orchestra conductor had given the signal, and then they all stop as abruptly after a few minutes.

For the fun of it, I walk over to the Landcruiser and blow the horn. The beetles stop their noisy song immediately. "How's that for competition?" I challenge them, while selecting two of the most appetizing looking cans from the remaining tinned food. Not finding the tin-opener, my trusty knife exposes lunch – it needs sharpening anyway. Back under the shade I find that bees have claimed the rest of my beer. They're amazingly quick; the hive must be close-by. "Well, let them have it." In this heat I'm in no mood for a quarrel; African bees are considered to be more aggressive than European species and I move the chair about ten feet, or three meters away. I'm about to scoop a spoonful of tuna fish when the sun beetles start up again.

******

The Kalahari is the largest continuous stretch of sand in the world. It starts in the northern parts of the Cape Province of South Africa, comprises about two thirds of western Botswana and more than a third of Namibia, and continues through eastern Angola, western Zimbabwe and the southern parts of Zambia. Sparsely populated by humans due to its inhospitality and size, it is a mysterious place with many archeological and other secrets still to be discovered. It is called a desert, but in fact it is covered with hardy species of grass, shrubs and trees. Arid as it is, nature has adapted many species of mammals, reptiles, insects and birds to survive and even flourish under the extreme climatic conditions of the '*Kgalakgadi*', as its native inhabitants, the '*Batswana*' call it.

Within the *Kgalakgadi* is the *Okavango Delta*, consisting of 16,000 square kilometers or 9,500 square miles of lush vegetation, crystal-clear waterways and pristine wildlife, considered one of the last vestiges of the animal kingdom. If you travel through it in a dugout canoe called a '*makoro*', you'll be convinced that the *Okavango* must have been the original Garden of Eden. The Kalahari also holds the secret to the '*Makgadikgadi*': 6,000 square kilometers or 3,500 square miles of flat salt pans, the vastness best appreciated from a place called Kubu Island, also known as 'the Lost City'. This island must have been named ages ago, for '*Kubu*' means hippo in the local languages. Although there are many telltale signs of a large lake in the past, no hippo could survive there today.

Several years ago my wife Tilla and I tried to find the Lost City and almost gave up after two days, experiencing just how treacherous the white clay crust of the *Makgadikgadi* was. Mid-morning on the third day we saw the island – like a mysterious mirage looming in the distance. Before reaching it, however, the adrenaline level in my blood stream was raised quite significantly: Our four-wheel drive would break through the pan's hard crust into a soggy, sticking, salty black clay, bogging it down to the extent that I had to make wide U-turns back to firm ground. To stop and try to go back was a mistake, as I learned very quickly. At one stage we spent four hours digging the vehicle out of the mud, then slowly reversed it back onto its tracks, where after I stayed on the edges of the pan.

Negotiating the last few kilometers across the pan to the Island felt like eternity. Finally reaching it, we set up camp and explored it on foot. Finding the Lost City was like treading on holy ground and feeling like taking off one's shoes. Being there, surrounded by silence with grotesquely gnarled baobab trees, guarding mysteries of eons gone by, instilled in us a feeling that is difficult to describe. It was like communicating without words, intensely, with age-old spirits still present in the ruins.

******

Glancing at the beer can, by then swarming with bees, I decided on a drink of water. Taking an enameled tin mug, I walked to the front of the vehicle, only to find something interesting but at the same time confusing. The canvas water bag, which I always hang over the winch in front of the vehicle, was covered with bees. It looked like the whole hive decided to claim it and was trying to carry it away.

"Now what?" I mumbled. Apart from being thirsty, the winch was probably the only thing that would pull me out of the mess.

"OK you guys," I decided, "that's **my** water, and I certainly don't feel like lukewarm water from the back of the truck."

Expecting to cause a war I stepped forward, but at the same time, hoping to negotiate and compromise for peace. Ever so gently, I pulled the cork from the top of the water bag. The bees were all over it but none of them seemed aware of my presence. I got hold of the bottom of the bag, slowly tilted it and filled the mug.

"No problem so far." A few bees landed on my hand. I changed hands, carefully. Flicking them off, I stepped back.

"This is interesting," I told myself. They didn't care about anything but the water, or for that matter, the moisture on the outside of the bag. Sipping cool water, I marveled at the wonder of one's mind, for the scene brought back many memories. During my final year at school, I did a biology project on bees and those little insects have fascinated me ever since.

Having some knowledge of their behavior and remembering how many times they had stung me, I realized that the hive could not be more than a few hundred meters away. Curiosity got the better of me and I started to follow their flight to and from the water source. Hoping to videotape their communication dance at the hive, I took the camera and started off in the general direction back to the hive. Any bee that discovers a substantial source of food or water will fly straight back to its hive and perform a dance at the entrance by buzzing and flipping its wings, running in circles and figure-of-eights, jumping up and down and generally displaying what we humans consider to be ludicrous behavior. This secret dance however, tells the other bees exactly what the treasure is and where to find it, without the original discoverer showing the way. They fly in a radius of up to ten kilometers or more than six miles from their hive in search of food. That they discovered my beer can and water bag so quickly was a strong clue that the hive was nearby.

As I walked through thorny shrubs and half dried grass, trying to follow the flight path of black specks in the sky, I was suddenly accompanied by a small bird with the opposite name: it was a greater honey guide, commonly found throughout Southern Africa. These birds are known to direct the honey badger and other mammals including man to beehives. The honey badger is exceptionally tough and raiding every hive it finds, invariably leaves enough honeycomb 'crumbs' for the honey guide bird to feast on.

With no intention of raiding the hive, it felt like I was just using the little bird, which fluttered in front of me from shrub to shrub, while uttering a sound like a shaken matchbox. I knew that I just had to follow it – once it perched on a tree or shrub without moving on, the hive would be within ten meters. So it was. About 400 meters from the vehicle the bird flew into the branches of a large camel thorn tree, whose trunk and bark was gnarled and twisted from two to three hundred years of existence. From the safety of the high branches, the honey guide hopped around very expectantly, now uttering a cry that sounded like 'Victoree... victoree...'

Underneath the tree the ground was trampled by antelope and other animals seeking its shade or, during the dry seasons, looking for the nourishment of its pods.

The hive was about 12 feet or four meters up, in a hollow branch. There was no chance of using the camera unless I climbed the tree.

"Too bad – and bad luck for you too, little honey guide." Not getting the expected reaction from me, he jumped lower and lower and almost frantically pointed at the entrance.

There is an old superstition (or is it the truth?) that if you do not leave some honey combs for the bird, the next time it will lead you to a python or poisonous snake or to dangerous predators. The reminder of this belief made me aware of where I was: in the middle of a vast wilderness of sand, overgrown by thorny shrubs and trees like the acacia I stood under, where every living thing has to succumb to the one and only law of nature: 'survival of the fittest'.

Although used to the bush, I felt a sudden uneasiness. I was far from the safety of the vehicle and had nothing with me but my knife and the camera. Looking round I saw nothing of concern, but had that funny feeling that something or somebody was watching me...

I was about to turn back, when I noticed something. Next to the trunk of the tree a few stones of tennis ball size were placed in a neat circle 18 inches, half a meter in diameter, some on top of the others. Having had some knowledge of the Bushmen's ways, I realized that those stones marked ownership of the hive in the first place, and of course that there were some Bushmen around. To tamper with a marked beehive means trouble. 'San' people, as they are also known, have little in life and are not concerned with possessions, but when they claim a beehive, beware – you may end up the target of a poisoned arrow! Alerted, I inspected the ground around the tree. Sure enough, a number of small human footprints were all around it, but days old. Then, covering some of them, was something of immediate concern – fresh lion tracks!

According to my own experience of the bush (which at the time I thought to have been more than average), the tracks had probably been made the previous night or early that morning.

"Nothing to be alarmed about," I mumbled and then continued to calm myself: "Obviously, like the other animals, lions must frequent the shade of this tree at midday."

Realizing that it was still hot, I may just as well have stumbled upon a pride dozing there. Those tracks were too fresh for comfort and too big for my futile attempt at positive thinking – they must have been left by one of the notoriously big black-maned Kalahari lion. The spoor of each front paw belittled my spread-out hand, and I was used to people remarking on the size of my hands...

Pretending not to be scared, I suppressed a strong urge to run (that would have been stupid) and started to walk slowly towards the vehicle. Constantly looking sideways and over my shoulders to ensure that no bush concealed any lion, I nervously made my way back. By then I had no intention other than to make camp for the night, cook myself a decent meal and to sleep. It had been a rough day and I had had enough of it.

Back at the vehicle with an hour of sunlight left, I wondered why I had felt so scared half an hour or so ago. There was really no difference then, except that I was close to a mechanical vehicle bogged down in sand. It would seem that something material always gives us a sense of security: Yesterday I had passed two or three abandoned Bushmen shelters on the way. They were nothing more than flimsy structures of thin flexible poles forming simple domes, not higher than one and a half meters or five feet high and covered so sparsely with grass that they would not even keep the rain out. But then, in this part of the world rain is of little concern. Lack of it for a few seasons, however, leads to disaster.

My own dome tent was much bigger and definitely more bug proof than any Bushman's overnighting idea. It had built-in mosquito nets and was waterproof and, therefore, seemed safe from all sorts of things like elephants and lions. Within a few minutes I pitched the tent and started to gather firewood. Thirty meters from camp, as I picked up another log, a small steenbok ram startled me when he rushed from a thicket of Bushmen candles. He ran and jumped a few meters and then with a twitching tail, calmly started to browse as if he was going out for supper anyway.

Conditions had changed significantly. The heat had subsided and only one or two dust devils made their presence known. The sun disappeared behind some clouds and promised a magnificent sunset. The sun beetles must have found something better to do because they had stopped their noise. A herd of springbok grazed nearby, snorting at my presence but seemingly unconcerned. Not a breeze in the air. A bateleur eagle swooped low over the treetops followed by its mate. The sound of their wings was like that of fast flying glider planes whizzing through the air. Not once did the two of them so much as flap a wing. I glanced around –that unsettling feeling of being watched was still with me...

Taking an empty drink can I cut it in half, filled it with sand and poured petrol into it from one of the jerry cans.

"That's something else to worry about," I thought. Although I had enough fuel left for a full tank it would not suffice for 200 miles or 300 kilometers if the road condition didn't improve. I put the can lighter into a hollow in the sand, lit it and placed firewood over it. Not long afterwards the kettle was hanging from a tripod. Coffee would go down well. A little more fiddling around and camp was set up. There was one piece of steak left and I took it from the fridge. A tinned can or two later and I was ready to prepare a good meal; hot coals from the hard lead wood tree would do the trick in about an hour.

It was time to see how I was going to get the vehicle out in the morning. If I had to use the winch, then one of the spare wheels would have to be dug into the sand about 20 meters in front of the vehicle to serve as an anchor for the winch cable – there was no suitable tree to take the strain. Alternatively, I could dig sand away from the front wheels, then use the high-lift jack to lift the rear of the vehicle out of the hole, after which I may have been able to drive it forward (the front wheels being engaged in 4-wheel drive), so that it would fall off the jack and out of the hole. To do that the jack would have to be at the rear center of the vehicle, and of course, that was where the hole was. That meant that I would have had to dig sand away from underneath the vehicle's rear end and insert logs or something similar over the hole to serve as a base for the jack.

I thought it best to start early the next morning before it got hot again. Temperature changes in the Kalahari are drastic. It was getting chilly – hinting that the night would be cold. "Let's leave the effort for dawn."

The water was boiling and I made myself coffee. The chair was still underneath the umbrella thorn and I walked over to fetch it. Picking up the beer can I empty the remaining flat beer. A number of unfortunate bees lay drowned or drunk on the sand. It struck me that if it weren't for the fact that they had distracted me, I would probably have labored and sweated in the heat to get the vehicle out and that I could have been 40 kilometers further.

"So what – tomorrow is another day..."

Suddenly the unmistakable 'Ooooorrrrrmpf-oooorrrrmpf-ooorrrmpf-orrmpf- mpf-mpf' of a lion roaring nearby.

"Probably half a kilo away – or more," I consoled myself.

As the last 'mpf' died down the silence became more alarming than his roar. Almost as if he really was the king of the jungle (or rather desert), nothing made a sound. Yet it lasted for a few seconds only before he was challenged by 'the cry of the Kalahari': the laughing cry of a black-backed jackal rang across the sands and bush, answered by another closer to camp and then by one further away, all hopeful of a kill in order to scavenge something.

In some mysterious way my chair moved closer to the fire and I quickly got a light going to see what I was doing with the food. It was getting rather dark. With a fluorescent light running from the vehicle's cigarette lighter, all was OK again. I sat down and sipped my coffee. Lions are inquisitive animals and I could've expected a visitor to drop by, judging from the distance of his roar. Flames from the campfire were flickering high, casting eerie shadows. I decided it needed another piece of wood or two – just for the sake of it.

A breeze rustled the dry leaves, followed by a gush of wind throwing dust in my eyes. I closed them and waited a few seconds. Nothing unusual, just a dust devil with no manners. Silence again. I lit a cigarette and relaxed. Another sip only to find a dry mopane leaf inside the mug. I reached for a twig, flicked it out and then lost myself staring at the fire.

"***Dumela Ra***!"

The words startled me silly and I spilled half the coffee. Looking up in fright, disbelieving my ears and half-blinded by leaping flames, I made out a small but dimly lit human shape, just across the fire in front of me. As my eyes adjusted themselves to the light (that's what I believed at the time), the figure slowly became clearer. It was an old Bushman. Still shocked, I wondered why he greeted me in Se'Tswana, the local language of the Batswana tribes. Stuttering, I returned his greeting with the same words, which simply mean 'I greet you Sir', and got up.

"*Ho'kai?*" he said smiling, which means 'Are you here?'

"Strange", I thought – that's the Northern Sotho's version of the greeting.

"*Ke gona*," I answered, 'I am.'

"*Le na ke gona*," he replied, 'And I am too.' Then he held out his right hand, with his left clasping his right arm just below the elbow. That was the Batswana's way again. I took his hand with my right, clasping my right arm with my left hand in the same place as he did. It is a sign of respect. We then released the grip of our right hands and each took hold of the other's thumb. But the old man didn't let go of my thumb as is customary, holding onto it until I felt uncomfortable.

This gave me the time to look him over. He was very old, judging from his white hair and wrinkled face. The skin of his body was creased from years in the sun and tanned a pale golden-brown to black. Small and skinny, he looked almost fragile. Except for a flimsy animal skin around his waist he was naked. I noticed two spears on the ground next to him.

"When did he put them down there?" I thought, but something else bewildered me: I found it difficult and embarrassing to look him straight in the face. His eyes looked like those of most Bushmen, deep dark pools of innocence, but his emitted a bluish-gray light, like tempered steel. They penetrated my very soul.

Eventually he let go of my thumb requesting: "*Ke nyaka metsi*," which means: 'I'd like some water', and sat down on the ground next to the fire.

"Peculiar," I thought. I showed respect by standing up when he greeted me and he showed respect by sitting down, as is their custom. "People are funny..."

I fetched the canvas bag, then without the bee problem, rinsed the forgotten coffee from my mug and poured him some water. He took the mug with both hands and sipped the water noisily, taking a long time. Fascinated, I thought about the fact that I had actually hoped to encounter some Bushmen on that route. That was the reason I took it in the first place. There are only 5000 or so real San people left and I was hoping for a few photographs. I was lucky. It's almost impossible to find Bushmen unless they decide to come to you.

"Except that this old man is no ordinary Bushman," I decided after a few minutes. It may have been reflections from the fluorescent light or from the flaming fire but before then I had never seen a Bushman with such startling eyes. Handing the mug back to me, he smiled and asked:

"Do you speak English?"

Surprised at his question, I replied: "Yes, and you do too?"

"*Aowa*," he said (meaning no or false) and continued: "But it will not be necessary, for we will understand each other."

Knowing only the basic words of Se'Tswana and thinking of how we would communicate if he didn't speak English, I suddenly realized what he had just said and how he said it.

"Impossible – cannot be," I mumbled to myself. Not believing my own ears, I asked him again if he spoke English.

"*Aowa*, but I told you we would understand each other..."

It is difficult to describe my astonishment at the time. The old man was talking to me in '*Khoisan*', with all the colorful clicking and clacking sounds of his native language and dialect. I had no knowledge of it whatsoever, yet I understood what he was saying. Realizing that sent a chill down my back and my skin turned gooseflesh. For the sake of saying something but not believing that he would understand, I pointed to the Landcruiser.

"Problem with car – fall into hole."

"*Eheh*," he replied. The word 'Eheh' means 'yes', 'I know' or is simply used to express affirmation or the truth. After a second or two he continued:

"It's no problem, we'll make a plan tomorrow. And do not worry how you speak to me – I understand." He carried on: "Why didn't you take honey from the hive this afternoon?"

He was definitely speaking the Bushmen language. Half my mind was trying to figure out how it was possible to understand him and the other half wouldn't believe it, but I replied anyway: "I… I saw that it belonged to somebody else and I wasn't hungry."

"You saw the footprints of *Xi'tau*?" he half-stated, half-asked.

"Who is *Xi'tau*?" but somehow I knew the answer and my blood ran cold.

"That's him…" He pointed to the umbrella thorn. What I saw made me freeze. Underneath the tree, barely ten meters away, lay a magnificent black-maned Kalahari lion, his eyes reflecting bright yellow in the light.

Before I could come to my senses the old man calmly said:

"He is my friend."

"Your f-f-friend?"

"*Eheh*, and don't be so scared – he won't come closer because he doesn't know you… yet."

"Must be dreaming; this is unreal," I thought.

"*Aowa*, *Xi'tau* is alive and very real," he remarked.

I definitely didn't say a word. How did he know what I was thinking? Who was this old man?

Staring at the lion, I calmed down slightly and as a safari tour leader, recalled that on many occasions, lion, elephant and other supposedly dangerous animals had walked through our camps. They never bothered us, to the extent that we would not even get up from our chairs if an elephant favored the leaves of a tree ten meters away or decided to drink our leftover dishwashing water.

That was something different though. What I experienced that evening was not normal. Still not knowing how to react, I said to the old man:

"My name is Uys, what is yours?"

"I am called Teecha," he answered. "How do you do, Ace?"

"I don't really know... But it's nice meeting you, Teecha."

The lion gave a big yawn and rolled over onto its back. Stretched out, with one hind and one forepaw held relaxed in the air, he was actually snoring. Xi'tau was the biggest lion I had ever seen...

******

18

THE BUSHMAN

We search for the meaning of life
in many different ways and in far away places.
We think that we'll find it through
recognition, fame, power, riches and security.
Once we achieve those, the answer to our reason for being
still eludes us and we keep on searching.
We end up disillusioned and confused.

If lucky, someday we meet someone who
puts us back onto the track, who shows us
that things are really simple and who helps us
to understand what we in fact already now.
We then realize that what we were searching for,
the greatest treasure in life,
is free and always within reach.

******

If ever I experienced and at the same time clearly understood the meaning of 'crazy mixed-up kid', it was that evening. I stared at the lion, then at Teecha and back at the lion. Trying to make sense, my mind raced through the past, searching for something to justify the situation and to put me back in control. At first it found nothing. In fact, it told me that I was nuts. However, retrieved from deep down in the subconscious something did come to the fore: maybe it was a survival instinct, an inquisitive trait, Teecha's apparent calmness or a realization that there are many things of which we know nothing. Whatever it was took control and managed to relax my tightly strung nerves.

Teecha sat cross-legged on the ground and stared at the flames of the fire. His calmness was catchy and my pulse must have slowed down considerably. I was still wondering whether I had actually breathed during the last minute or two when he got up and walked straight towards Xi'tau.

"Teecha, No!" I shouted. "Come back!" My warning fell on deaf ears, he didn't even bother to look back. He walked on and picked up a skin-bag, which he must have left right where Xi'tau was lying. The lion just continued to snore.

Back at the fire, as if we had known each other for many years he said fellow-like: "Come Ace, let's prepare some food..."

"OK" I agreed, but not at all in control of myself as my shaking legs were the give-away. But it was not from fear I think – rather the reality of the situation, which touched both body and soul.

If I was scared (and most certainly I was) then that emotion made way for something else, something I had never experienced before. For a fleeting instant I knew all the answers, knew everything about life, creation and existence. No matter how much I think about that emotion today, I just cannot find the words to describe it. Something like '*Eureka*!' I thought at the time. However, at that very instant I lost my newly found knowledge again. Just like a flashbulb fuses, I was enlightened for a split second, knowing it all, only to feel like a kid who dropped his ice-cream on the beach without having a lick. No matter how I tried to grope for it, that knowledge would not come back.

I must have looked very puzzled for Teecha said:

"Don't worry about it Ace, one day you'll know again..."

That fueled my bewilderment: I hadn't said a word to him about my lost revelation and was about to ask him about the lion. He responded to my thoughts before I had the time to formulate the question:

"White hunters shot Xi'tau, his two sisters and his mother, several rain seasons ago. The lioness and the other cubs were all killed but he managed to escape into an ant bear hole like the one your vehicle fell into. He was about four months old. I saw what happened and thought that he would die anyway. When the hunters left with their trophies, I decided to use his skin for a bag and dug him out of the hole. It took me a long time.

When I found him he was still alive but badly wounded. According to our habits, I would have killed him to put him out of misery, but *N!odima*, the spirit of life, told me to first consult my bones. I threw them and then *Gao!na* commanded me to help him instead. So I hunted a springbok and fed him. For some reason Xi'tau allowed me to tend his wounds. I hunted and brought him food for several weeks. That is how we became friends. When he was well again I taught him how to hunt and now we hunt together. He follows me wherever I go."

"Who is *Gao!na*?" I was fascinated by his story and tried to imitate the tongue click indicated by the '!'.

"The same God as yours."

From the way he answered I was supposed to have known it. While I contemplated his answer, he took several bulb-like roots from his skin bag, each about the size of a golf ball. He used a stick to scratch a few coals from the hot fire and then put three or four bulbs onto the coals. The rest he handed to me. "These are sand mushrooms – try them."

They had no resemblance to any mushroom I knew, but the reference made my mouth water. Slitting one open with my knife, its texture and smell was similar to a mushroom. I decided to try them fried in butter.

"Thanks." I got up to get a frying pan. At that stage everything felt completely normal and I continued preparing dinner. We chatted about this and that. Xi'tau stirred every now and then but it didn't bother me in the least. When I asked Teecha where he himself came from, he replied: "From the spirit of the San, to succour you." At the time I considered his reply as figure-of-speech, like many peoples in Africa express themselves. Later on though, I had to accept it as he intended. We had supper in silence. After a while I offered him some of my steak and he questioned with gratitude: "Beef?" and took the piece of meat with his fingers. He seemed to enjoy it thoroughly. In return he asked: "How are the mushrooms?

They were delicious, actually better tasting than the kind I knew and I asked him where he got them from. "I'll show you tomorrow," was all he said.

"Coffee?"...

"*Eheh*." While I made it he asked: "Do you have a rifle?"

"No, I used to hunt but not anymore. That is my latest rifle..." and I pointed to the video camera, thinking that he probably wouldn't even know what it was.

"Good."

From his question, I assumed that he wanted me to shoot him some game and his comment was unexpected.

"Do you hunt, Teecha?" Immediately I thought: "Stupid question, asking that of a Bushman." He replied almost tactfully: "*Eheh*, when I'm hungry. If you want to, I'll show you what it means to hunt." I was about to tell him that I knew enough about hunting but then pondered his words. What did he mean? Traditionally, Bushmen hunt with a bow and poisoned arrows. I hadn't seen his bow yet and asked him about it.

"I don't need one."

"How come?"

"You'll see."

Surprised at his answer, I left it at that.

It was bedtime and getting rather cold. A little unsure of his preferences, I asked Teecha if I could pitch him another tent for the night. "*Aowa*, I sleep here." "It will be cold – do you want a blanket?" "Not to worry, I'll be fine." With that, I decided to turn in. "Goodnight Teecha, and thanks for the mushrooms."

"Thanks for the beef – I'll see you in the morning."

I slipped into my sleeping bag, zipped up the tent's fly screen but left the flap open. From where I lay on the air mattress I could see Teecha's silhouette in the glow of the coals, still sitting in the same position.

It felt as if I had just dozed off, when something woke me again. What time was it? In the light of a penlight torch my watch showed 4am. Half asleep, I realized where I was and that I must have dreamt it all. A glance through the tent flap, just to make sure. No, it wasn't a dream. Teecha was still sitting by the fire in the same position. He stirred, then reached out and put another log on the fire, which sent sparks flying through the air. I leaned back again. "Was this really true?..." At the same time I heard what actually woke me: a spotted hyena continued his spine-chilling cry close-by: '*Whoo-oop, whoo-oop, whoo-oop*'... followed by a cackling laugh that could only be described as that of a witch brewing her favorite stew.

Teecha didn't move and I pulled the sleeping bag over my shoulders. When I woke again it was light. This time it was the loud crowing of a Swainson's francolin cock that told me a new day had arrived. His harsh '*Kwahli! Kwahli! Kwahli*!' rang through the bush, worse than any alarm clock.

"Right, time to move on."

I unzipped the fly screen and was about to crawl out when a vision of *Xi'tau* crossed my mind. That didn't really make a difference but caused me to stick my head out first, deciding that perhaps it was a good thing to do when you're in the bush. The fire was going and a boiling kettle hung from the tripod. Nobody in sight though. A glance at the acacia tree showed no lion. I stood up and stretched. A little worried about where to attend to nature's early morning call, I scrutinized the surroundings but saw nothing dangerous. Walking around to the other side of the vehicle I watered a particularly dry looking plant.

Coffee would be great. With a steaming mug and emboldened by coppery golden rays creeping through the bush, I walked to the tree where Xi'tau had been sleeping. I definitely hadn't dreamt him either. The big tracks that I had seen the day before were his. I went back to the fire, sat down and warmed my hands around the mug while sipping from it. A slight breeze stirred. This time a cheerful "*Dumela Ra*" prevented me from spilling the coffee. With a broad smile, Teecha held up a dead guinea fowl and said: "Breakfast."

Returning his greeting I said: "That will be nice, but I cannot stay much longer – I must pack up and leave."

At that stage I still don't know whether I felt his disappointment or saw it in those eyes, but I experienced a strange feeling. Trying to rid my mind of it, I asked him how he managed to get the guinea fowl.

"From a trap I had set yesterday," and he started to pluck the feathers.

Still sensing something weird and that he didn't approve of my leaving I tried to change the subject: "Would you like some coffee?" and after a nod I poured him some. Handing him the mug, I wanted to know about Xi'tau.

"Oh, he's around – he wouldn't go too far without me."

Then he said: "You ask many questions, Ace – don't you know about things?"

Taken aback, I didn't answer him but contemplated his statement. I certainly knew a lot more about life, the world and the sciences than he did – I must even know about some things he had never heard of. Yet right then I was not so sure. Without any further thought I asked him:

"What do **you** know, Teecha?"

"Enough."

On the spur of the moment I asked once more: "Teecha, how old are you?"

Expecting an answer like 'eighty summers', he surprised me again:

"I don't care – it wouldn't make a difference..."

Suddenly I had no haste. We baked the guinea fowl, seasoned with various spices, in a cast-iron pot over the coals, and had a feast. Teecha smacked his tongue and licked his fingers repeatedly, silent except for an occasional smile that showed a row of well kept teeth. That also amazed me. Surely at his age and with no dentist around he should have been almost toothless.

Flicking the last bone away I reminded myself: "Get back to reality."

I got up, took a spade and started to dig sand away from the Landcruiser's front wheels. Teecha watched me in silence but I was certain his look spelled disapproval of my effort. Already sweating, I asked him if he'd mind finding some logs to put across the hole in order to support the high-lift jack.

"That won't be necessary."

I looked up and was sure he wiped a smile off his face. Annoyed I started sarcastically: "You have a better idea? How the hell else do you think ..." but he interrupted bluntly: "No problem Ace – I push you out if you start car."

I laughed and suddenly he looked offended. Yet there was no way a frail old Bushman could have had any effect in trying to push that Landcruiser out.

"Stupid old man," I mumbled but at the same time felt sorry at his lack of common sense. Before I could explain why his suggestion would not work, he commanded: "Ace, get into your vehicle and start it!"

At that very instant Xi'tau appeared and flopped down about 25 meters way, as if to witness the action. He stared at me with large yellow eyes, expectantly... It is difficult to describe the mixture of emotions I felt right then. Thoughts like: "Ignorance is bliss, old fool" and "With that lion around, I'll be better off inside the vehicle than out of it", crossed my mind. At the same time I decided that Teecha might learn something about vehicles weighing a few tonnes. But I also remembered that he was still speaking to me with those clickety-clack sounds of his mother tongue. Maybe that, the presence of Xi'tau or just the fact that time and reality didn't seem to matter much, forced me into the truck. Maybe it was the tone of Teecha's voice or Xi'tau's eyes. I didn't know and couldn't care.

Teecha walked to the back of the vehicle. Fumbling with the keys, I eventually got it started and shifted into gear. As if I believed that a little shove might do the trick, I shouted back through the window: "Push!" and put my foot down. Expecting screeching tyres and only to sink deeper into the sand, I was about to experience the supernatural: the rear of the vehicle just lifted and in the next second both machine and I shot forward. Some instinct caused me to act reasonably normal but I released the clutch before switching off anyway, stopping with a jerk.

I jumped out. Teecha stood way back, several meters on the other side of the hole. He hadn't so much as touched the vehicle – I just knew it. "See, *hakuna matata*" – Swahili for 'no problem' – he remarked smiling, and waved his hand nonchalantly in the air.

Speechless, I leaned onto the open door and stared at him for a long time. "You will stay for a day or two?" he asked as if lifting a fully laden 4-wheel drive out of an ant bear hole was indeed no problem.

After what felt like searching for something well known but totally lost, and then upon finding it realizing that that something was myself, I solemnly promised: "Yes, if you'll teach me what you know."

"Then let me show you where to get mushrooms."

With that, he picked up his spears and skin-bag and started for the bush.

I glanced at my watch: It was Wednesday April 16, just past 9 o'clock in the morning. By then I figured that Teecha could not have been the average Bushman. He must have been one of their leaders or medicine men with unusual knowledge like the *sangomas* or witch doctors of black tribes are claimed to have. I was indeed lucky – if I played my cards right this old man might just give me some insight into their superstitious beliefs, practices and use of unknown powers. As usual, when I spend some time in the bush, I removed my watch and put it inside the vehicle's glove compartment. With a spirit heightened by the excitement of adventure, I took my knife, cigarettes and camera and shouted to Teecha: "Wait for me! I'm on my way…"

******

For the next few days I was the pupil, led by a master of nature and life. For every question I asked, Teecha had one or more answers accompanied by vivid gestures, imitations of animals and clicking/clacking of the tongue. He used his digging stick to scratch diagrams and pictures on the sand to explain some tale or concept. Some of his ideas and answers made sense, some challenged my principles and beliefs. The things he showed me about nature itself opened my eyes to a different Kalahari than the one I thought I knew. I was at first astonished by his knowledge of just about any animal or plant we came across, then more so when I realized that he knew more about science, psychology and life in general than everything I have studied and read about, combined.

The rest of this book tries to explain some of the things he told me and what had happened in the next few days. My questions about life and existence couldn't have been that different from most of us. I feel compelled to share his thoughts with you. Hopefully they will get all of us thinking a bit more about life, ourselves and others – and, I sincerely hope that one day, you too will meet somebody like Teecha.

THE FIRST DAY

As we walked through patches of acacia trees, around thorny shrubs and over seemingly endless sand ridges I was constantly aware of a rather big cat following us. *Xi'tau* walked when we walked and rested in the shade of some tree or shrub whenever we did. However, he kept his distance, always fifty to a hundred meters away. Somehow his presence made me feel rather safe, so to speak. Little else in the Kalahari could be more dangerous, and with someone like him on your side, who had to fear? It was like having a strange guardian angel around who shook his shabby black-maned head from time to time to rid himself of flies. In the midday heat those plaugesome little insects became a real nuisance.

Walking on foot with no rifle across your shoulder and no droning vehicle to block your hearing, it was astounding to find how much more one became aware of day to day life in the Kalahari. I could hear the wind through the grass, birds chirping, animals snorting at our approach and a medley of insect overtures.

Teecha reminded me a few times to walk more softly and I tried my best to do so. His bare feet made no sound at all. Two or three times I stopped and let him walk on, trying to hear his footsteps and to figure out how he managed to move so quietly. "Must be my boots," I eventually consoled myself, and decided that when we stopped again I'd take them off.

My perception of silence, awareness and movement must have slowly changed. I started hearing strange noises and noticed much more around me. When at any time I asked: "Teecha, what was that?" he would respond: "Oh, she's *One-Ear*" or "That's *Scatter-bones* – he's plain silly," or something to that effect. He seemed to know every animal and bird individually by name and recognized them even by the tracks they left. It didn't take me too long to get the message and I started asking: "Who was that?"

When I asked how or why an animal got its name, Teecha would relate a colorful story about it. "I once tried to hunt him down..." and he pointed to a thicket of '*vaalbos*' trees. I stared at the 'gray bush' as the name implies but saw nothing. "Who and where?"

"It's *Play-around-the-bush*; he's looking straight at you."

Not knowing who or what to look for, I stared intensely in the direction he pointed and saw only *vaalbos*. I was about to give up, when a kudu bull moved slightly, just enough for his horns to glitter in the sun. I first saw the horns and face, then gradually his neck and then the whole body. He was so well camouflaged, no more than 30 meters away, that I would never have seen him but for Teecha.

Speaking softly, he said: "Ace, you will have to learn to recognize shapes instead of colors if you want to survive here – and for that matter, if you want to survive anywhere. Colors are deceptive: you must also learn to recognize a man by the shape of his heart and not his color."

I was still trying to grasp what he had just told me when he whispered: "OK, you stay here and I'll show you his name."

"Show me his name?" I asked quietly, not sure whether I had heard him correctly.

"Eheh." Then Teecha vanished. In the next few seconds he was ten meters closer to the kudu, which calmly kept on browsing.

As Teecha disappeared completely between the shrubs, the kudu was immediately on the alert. He stood motionless with big rounded ears pointing straight at me, and the next instant he fled, without panic. I heard what sounded like: 'ku-du, ku-du, ku-du', as he trotted quietly to the other side of the bush. From nowhere, Teecha appeared on my side and started to stalk around the bush towards the left. The buck was gone. In the next few seconds though, 'ku-du, ku-du' once more and the antelope came trotting round from the right in full sight, without so much as a glance in my direction. All his attention and his big ears were focused on the bush. He stopped, turned and trotted anti-clockwise again. Teecha appeared in view, spear in hand.

This beating around the bush continued for at least five minutes and became rather amusing. Teecha acted with his spear in a really serious fashion, smiling at me whenever he appeared on my side of the vaalbos and then tiptoeing to the right or left, trying to outwit the kudu. When the antelope decided he had had enough of the game he crashed though the surrounding grass and thorn-shrubs, stopping briefly on top of a small dune to look back before disappearing. His long spiral horns made at least three and a half turns – a trophy hunter's dream... "See, that is his name." I must have been so preoccupied in thought that Teecha startled me once more. He appeared next to me in complete silence.

"Dammit, Teecha, don't do this to me, you'll frighten me stiff."

"Ace, had I been anything like Xi'tau or Half-tail the leopard, you would have been stiff," he replied dryly.

"OK, I get the message," I said laughing, "but next time please say something before you fall out of thin air."

I wanted to ask him about Half-tail but his sudden appearances was of more concern. "By the way Teecha, how do you manage to do it?"

"*Tchi... tchi*," he uttered; "You're easy prey – constantly off-guard, daydreaming or worrying about trivial issues. You haven't yet told your mind to observe and to be on the alert, even when you are busy with something else. Do it, and you'll be surprised at the things it'll tell you. As for me falling out of the sky, I need to be a part of the bush, so I become part of the bush, I *am* the bush. I don't tell myself 'I am the bush, I am the bush' – I *know* I am the bush, that's why you do not see me. It doesn't help telling yourself that you are something you know you do not want to be, or that you want something you know you do not really need. You must *know* things."

Teecha's words were somewhat confusing and I missed the point of his explanation. Maybe he had hit so hard and deep that my mind discarded everything he said as useless information, so I asked him: "Will you ever kill the kudu, Teecha?"

"His name is Play-around-the-bush; will *you* kill him?"

He sounded upset with me. I felt rather silly but managed to stutter: "N…no, certainly not."

"You ask some good questions Ace, but others are stupid."

I decided to think before asking him anything but to no avail – my next question was out long before I had the time to think it over: "Teecha, what does it mean to *know* things?"

When he didn't answer me I wondered whether that was another stupid one. Not knowing what to do next, I sat down in the shade of a small tree and started taking off my boots.

"Why are you doing that?"

"So I can walk more quietly, like you."

"It's not your boots, it's the way you walk and I don't think that will help you at all – you'll end up making more noise."

This time I became upset and thought: "I'll show you, old man." I tied the laces together, slung the boots over my shoulder and set off. I had barely walked ten meters when I had enough reasons to reconsider my idea: The sand was extremely hot and automatically I walked faster. In the next ten meters my feet were burning and my legs started acting like those of a cat on a hot tin roof. Ten more meters and Teecha's warnings were of no importance.

"Shade!" a commanding little voice shouted and desperately I looked around for the nearest tree. Relief was another 30 meters away and I made a dash for it. In the process, I didn't care much how I reached the shade, so I got my pants torn by hook-thorn shrub and screamed "Ouch!" at least three times as thorns penetrated deep into the soles of my feet. I hop-skip-and-jumped the last ten meters, fell down in the shade and started pulling thorns from my burning feet.

A funny noise made me look up. Teecha was still standing where I had left him, bending over forward, with his arms across his wrinkled belly and screaming with laughter. It took me a while to accept the fact that I must have made good subject material for a comedy. As Teecha came walking towards me he couldn't control himself and burst into laughter a few more times. His eyes were streaming with tears, he had a silly look on his face and he kept on making funny noises. Eventually I realized that he tried his best not to laugh and my own sense of humor saved the situation, as I burst out laughing too. He fell down next to me and we laughed our hearts out. After a while Teecha got up, wiped the tears from his face and said: "Ace, you really made my day. Now put your boots back on and let me teach you how to walk.

"First of all, with every step you take you put your toes and the ball of your foot down first – not your heel like you do: Like this..."

He pointed his foot forward but at the same time slightly downward, so that his toes touched the ground before his heels did. He continued demonstrating: "As soon as your foot touch the ground in this way, your knee must be slightly bent with your body leaning forward, so that your full weight comes down on your whole foot every time. This way you are always completely balanced, the softness of your whole foot absorbing the shock of your body weight with each step.

"You will also find that you do not need to swing your arms forward and backward to balance yourself, leaving them free to carry something and you use less energy."

He walked to and fro a few times. For the first time I realized that he moved quite quickly with little body movement other than his legs, giving the impression that he floated. And, though he was a mere five meters away, I couldn't hear a sound.

"Come, give it a go," he said.

I felt like a child taking his first steps, looking for approval from his parents. "Eheh, that's right," or "Aowa, bend more forward," Teecha instructed. It felt awkward at first but not too difficult to do when I concentrated.

"Right, now a little faster, and keep your arms still."

It wasn't long before I thought I had the hang of it and noticed with surprise that I could hardly hear my own footsteps. Eager to test-drive myself, I said: "OK, I'm ready – let's go."

"Not so fast, Ace. The next thing you must learn to do is to walk behind yourself."

"Walk behind myself? How the heck is that possible?" I was more than skeptical.

"Have you ever noticed how dogs and cats walk through obstacles so that their hind feet step in the exact spots where their front feet did?"

"Yes, that's quite clever but they don't walk behind themselves?"

"In a way they do, because they do not look to see where they will put their hind feet down next, they already know. In the same way you must look ahead, finding all the best spots to step on and you must put your feet down exactly there. The faster you move, the further ahead you plan your way. It's like taking a detail snapshot of your route every five meters or so of the next ten meters. It must become second nature to you and that takes time. That's how you walk behind yourself – so you don't step on dry twigs or leaves, into thorns or on snakes. "You must do the same on your path of life but that's something I can only tell you to do. You'll have to train yourself and it will be much more difficult than walking in the bush." He turned around unceremoniously and walked on.

To change your ways is never easy. I followed Teecha with good intentions and really concentrated. "Ball of the foot first, bend slightly forward, look ahead, don't step on dry leaves". Then I remembered that I should have kept my arms still. "Knees slightly bent, keep the balance, find the best spots to step on, not my heels first, snapshot ahead, Oops!" – straight into a sickle bush. "This way around, now look 20 meters ahead – click – where's Teecha?" 'Crunch, crunch' went my heels in the sand and 'Crack!' as a twig snapped. "Dammit!"

"Keep at it Ace, you're doing fine." His voice came from behind me, adding fuel to frustration. "I told you it would take time – now follow me."

That helped a great deal as he led the way, leaving me to concentrate on how to walk. I literally followed in his footsteps. Where the terrain was smooth, his steps were fairly evenly spaced, but erratic through long grass or around shrubs and thorns. Yet it still looked as though he himself floated on air and never once did I see him looking at his feet.

After walking a few more minutes in silence, Teecha suddenly stopped. "Mushrooms," he said, and held up his hand as if we were hunting some elusive animal.

I looked around but saw nothing. Nothing except sand, grass and bush. No mushrooms growing anywhere. He put his bag down, took his digging stick and started to open the sand almost by my feet. About four inches or ten centimeters deep he unearthed one of those delicious mushrooms. Then he pointed to another, less than six feet or two meters away and said: "Where the sand is cracked, like this, grows a mushroom."

There was a slight break in the sand's smooth windblown texture, which I would never have noticed. After a few unsuccessful and eventually successful tries of my own, I was just about to get carried away when Teecha said: "We need no more, we have enough for today. Let's go home."

Left on my own, I probably would have continued digging for mushrooms just to get more. His comment about having enough for the day made me think. Had I taken any more they would have been wasted because there was no way of preserving them. I also found his reference to the camp as 'home' rather intriguing.

That night we enjoyed butter-fried mushrooms once more. We talked and talked. I had almost forgotten about Xi'tau until he suddenly appeared and lay down, a little closer to the campfire this time than was comfortable. Moving my chair to get away from the smoke, I noticed the faintest of grins on Teecha's face.

We had both finished our meal when Teecha reached for his skin bag and produced what looked to me like a miniature bow and arrow. I knew that an adolescent male bushman used a tiny bow like that to shoot a small arrow into the bum of the young girl he fancies. If according to custom, she pulls it out and hands it back to him, they are immediately engaged to be married. However, if she breaks it and throws it away, she's not interested. Anyway, I was just starting to wonder what possible use someone of Teecha's age could have for such a bow, when he placed the one string end into his mouth, holding the bow with his left hand. With his right, he took what I thought was the arrow and started to swiftly scratch-rub the wood of the bow from one side to the other. At the same time he moved the bow to and fro like a mouth organ, so that the string moved from left to right between his lips.

All of the sudden the night turned quiet, as if everything else was as surprised as me to the tunes of his music. I could do nothing but listen. Soft, strangely weird yet beautiful tunes sounded into the silence. His cheeks billowed in and out, as if he was blowing into the instrument like a piper, but his lips were slightly parted. Fascinated to say the least, I watched and listened as he played. Some melodies were bright and cheerful, others sad and lonely, and Teecha was a real entertainer. Finishing his show, he stood up and bowed smiling to the left and right as if he had performed in Central Square. I stood up, clapped my hands and cheered. Xi'tau didn't approve of my noise and grunted defiantly at me, so I sat down again. Teecha grinned like earlier that evening and handed me the small bow and arrow, saying:

"This is probably as primitive as you'll find any musical instrument. You try it – it is called a *Se!warra'warra*."

At the time I didn't have the foggiest idea of how it worked except that I should put the string between my lips and scratch the bow with the arrow. In doing that, I noticed that the bow was notched all along the outside edge, the notches starting about half a millimeter apart on one end and ending into deeper notches approximately 3 millimeters apart on the other. By scratching the bow to and fro with the 'arrow' it caused the string to vibrate, and the trick was to use your mouth as a reverberating box, not by blowing onto the string as I had thought, but by increasing or decreasing the cavity of the mouth, using your cheeks and lips in any possible combination. Needless to say the first sounds I produced with that *Se!warra'warra* caused all nightlife to continue normally. What I soon learned, however, was that it produced the loudest sounds with your mouth almost shut, and the weakest with your mouth wide open. After some truly screeching false notes, I gave it up as a bad job and handed the instrument back.

The Kalahari on a cloudless night with no moon is an excellent place for stargazing. We were staring at the dying flames of the fire when out of the corner of my eye I saw a shooting star. It brightened the already starlit sky for a second before disappearing in a shower of sparks. Staring at the empty space where the meteor burnt out, I wondered if Teecha knew anything about stars. Looking for the Southern Cross, I noticed a bright and fast moving 'star', obviously a satellite or maybe a space shuttle. Pointing it out to Teecha, I asked him if he knew what it was. He glanced towards the sky but didn't answer me.

Waving my hand towards the heavens I asked: "Do you know where all that comes from and what it is?"

I silently hoped that he would share with me some of the Bushmen's superstitious folklore and tales about stars. His reply however, caught me completely off-guard: "Eheh, don't you?"

I had to think awhile before answering. I told him that I know something about stars, but that I wished I knew where they came from, how they were created and when it all happened. I mentioned that the origin of everything is a subject that always fascinated me and that none of the theories, religions and explanations I have studied made any real sense. I finally admitted: "No Teecha, I don't know how it came about, but please tell me what you know."

******

THE BEGINNING

It is said that the future lies in the hands
of those who dedicate their lives
to explore three infinities:
The infinitely big,
the infinitely small,
and the infinitely complex.
Yet to unravel the wonders and mysteries of these infinities requires the acceptance of a fourth: The infinitely simple.

******

"'*Dis maar net so,*'" Teecha replied in my mother tongue.

Only later did I realize how difficult it is to convey the true meaning of those few Afrikaans words to another language. My best translation is: "It is so just because it is". At the time, though, I frowned at his answer, but true to form decided there and then that he had obviously never thought about the universe and existence. A little disappointed, I asked: "Is that all you can say about stars?"

He remained silent. I mistook it that he had cleverly sidestepped his lack of knowledge and that he really wanted to know more. I was about to eagerly tell him how big and how far away stars actually are and what we know about them, when he calmly stated: "Ace, you promised to stay a few days and I promised to tell you what I know. What I've just told you is the first thing you should know about stars and for that matter, about everything else."

This time I detected wisdom in his voice that abruptly put an end to my enthusiasm. I was almost relieved for not blabbering away. Something told me that his answer was a simple truth, yet 'too simple' for me to understand. Confused, I asked him: "OK Teecha, then what do you mean with: '*Dis maar net so*'?"

He answered in a voice that compelled me to listen: "Ace, things are simple but that is the difficult part to accept. To make sense of your existence you have to explore and know many complex facts but you must never lose sight of the basic truths. For instance, if you only study the complicated physics of the universe, you'll end up nowhere. Likewise, if you accept everything around you for what it is without question, you're even closer to nowhere. You'll see what I mean, but first, something about stars..."

He pointed to the night sky. "As you know that misty cloud over there consists of millions and millions of stars. Sometimes, like tonight, you stare at it in wonder. What you often forget is that your sun is just another star, one amongst those millions in the Milky Way – your own galaxy. Besides the Milky Way there are many other galaxies in the universe. Each galaxy is a huge cluster of stars, similarly shaped or totally different to yours. You give names to individual stars and galaxies. You try to predict the future by observing the movement of planets and stars and you study them with all your state-of-the-art technologies. What do you get for all your efforts?"

I was about to tell him that at least we get closer to the truth, but learned instead that he had a way of answering his own questions:

"Eheh, Ace, you gain a little knowledge here and there, but most of the time you find even more astonishing and inexplicable mysteries. You discover there are millions of other galaxies out there as you try to map the heavens. You run out of names and start giving them codes, like 'NGC 3031', which is a spiral nebula or cloud of dust in Ursa Major. That is an Sb-type galaxy, which is similar to your own and to Andromeda. Take another, the Large Magellanic Star Cloud, which belong to the 'Local Group' of galaxies at a distance of 52 kilo parsecs. This star cloud contains about ten thousand million stars. There is the Virgo cluster of galaxies at a distance of 11 mega parsecs, which contains about two thousand five hundred galaxies. There is 'NGC 2623', two colliding galaxies in the star sign Cancer and there is 'Cygnus A', two other galaxies in collision..."

"That's incredible, Teecha," I interrupted. "Where did you learn all that? Did you just say Virgo consists of 2,500 galaxies?... and what is a 'parsec'?"

He answered my questions in part only: "Distances between stars are mind-boggling. A 'light year', which is a common term in scientific circles, is the distance that light travels in one year, at a speed of around three hundred thousand kilometers per second, which gives a distance of more or less six million million miles or close on ten million million kilometers. A parsec is three and a quarter times that distance, calculated from the trigonometric parallax of stars."

He remained silent for a moment, as if giving me time to absorb it. I felt like a spare wheel – my high school maths teacher must have slipped up on that one and all I could remark was: "That is far indeed."

Teecha made absolutely sure that I understood him:

"The closest other star to your own is Proxima Centauri, more than four light years from here. A kilo parsec is one thousand parsecs and a mega parsec one million parsecs. The Virgo cluster of galaxies is very, very far away. Imagine driving your vehicle something like 386,496,000,000,000,000,000 kilometers to get there. Traveling non-stop for 24 hours a day at an average speed of 100 kilometers an hour, it would take you 450 million million years to get there. That span of time is much more than the age of the universe, according to some of your scientists and astrophysicists."

By then I was astounded at Teecha's knowledge. I was partly aware of what he told me about through study, science fiction books and TV programs, but coming from a Bushman it was unreal. In fact, totally impossible according to common perception.

However, eager to learn something new, I realized that the key to it was to be found in his simple words: 'Dis maar net so'.

Impatient as always, I tried to draw it out of him: "That is indeed fascinating Teecha, but what did you mean with..."

He interrupted me as bluntly as I did him: "Be patient Ace, I'm getting there!" and calmly continued: "The first book in your Bible, Genesis, starts with: 'In the beginning...' That is certainly true of your own solar system (the sun, earth, moon and the other planets like Mars, Venus and Saturn), and even for your own galaxy. There had to be some beginning, as scientifically you've figured out that earth is approximately four and a half thousand million years old. Your minds are baffled by these 'astronomical' figures, but if earth's age can be determined then the words: 'In the beginning' are quite true. Not so, Ace?"

"Obviously," I conceded. He remained silent for a while, prodded at the fire with a stick and added more wood. I wanted to know: "Teecha, you talk about 'you' and 'yours' all the time – who are you referring to?"

"Mankind."

So far everything he said made sense but I knew he was leading me on to something else, and I wondered why he didn't say 'we' or 'ours'. I kept quiet and waited for him to continue:

"You know that there will be an end to earth and to your solar system. This has been prophesied all through the ages. If the end doesn't happen in your lifetime or within the next few thousand years, then naturally it would occur a few hundred million years from now, when your own sun will simply burn out and die. When that happens, earth will either be cindered to ashes or it will freeze up completely, with no light and heat to support any life. This depends on how your sun will die as that may happen in a number of ways. So, within the limits of your thinking and based on certain facts available to you, for earth there was a beginning and there will be an end."

He paused again and this time I used the opportunity: "Yes, that's all fine but how did everything start in the first place? – How can something start from nothing?"...

"That seems to bother many people, Ace." His reply was without any hesitation as if he had had to explain it many times before. "In fact, that same question is the reason why most religions exist. People find the idea of '*something from nothing*' unacceptable, that's why religions tell you that everything was created by a supreme being or God – but then who created Him?"

"Wait a second," I stopped him urgently, "now you're bordering on atheism and I do not accept that."

"Neither do I, Ace – will you let me finish?" He sighed.

"Sure, sure. Uhmm... Sorry," I apologized, thinking that I might have antagonized him.

Teecha stared at me for several seconds. His penetrating black eyes searched my deepest beliefs and suddenly I felt very nervous. He gave a comforting laugh and commanded: "Relax Ace, things are not that serious." I had to smile and that gave him the go ahead:

"Let me put it this way: atheists generally deny the existence of God and prefer the 'Solid State Theory', suggesting that there is no need to bring in a God as there is no need to explain a beginning nor an ending. They have a good point but they do not think it through. In contrast agnostics want to have everything explained logically or scientifically. They mostly believe in material hypotheses like the 'Big Bang' and in things like Richard Gott's 'Bubble theory', which supposedly created the universe, or in a 'Primordial Soup' from which life evolved."

At that stage I just had to interrupt: "Teecha, what you're telling me is probably true but how the hell do you know all this? Are you really a Bushman?" Flabbergasted, I didn't give him any time to answer and carried on: "Where did you learn about the Big Bang? What are you doing here?"

The very latest astronomical evidence supports the Big Bang theory and it is being hailed as the most important discovery this century. I could not accept the fact that Teecha seemed to know all about it and fired another question: "Do you have a radio or TV somewhere?"

When he answered me, it was in measured words:

"Ace, I'll be whatever your imagination wants me to be. And I only promised to tell you what I know, not how I came to know it."

His answer riled me but from the tone of his voice he meant what he said and I knew not to plague him further. "True – a deal is a deal," I succumbed, hoping that somehow he would give himself away. When he continued ignoring my escapade, I knew he wasn't going to.

"Scientists and religions are still no closer to the answer of what caused the universe to come into being than they were years ago. It would seem, though, that wise men from ages past knew more about this subject than your present day scientific gurus. Many prominent scientists are returning to the wisdom of ancient scriptures, hoping that those will throw more light on their investigations and calculations. An enormous amount of time and money is spent in trying to prove a beginning. They use all the latest number crunching computers and particle accelerators to do this, and although interesting discoveries are made in the process, NO beginning has yet been proved. It has been established, though, that the part of the universe you see with your eyes and even 'see' with sophisticated radio telescopes, is about fifteen thousand million years old."

I kept on listening.

"Observed facts show that the known universe is moving, expanding and apparently also cooling down. Physicists are able theoretically, to trace its origin back to where something like a Big Bang may have happened. This backtracking in time is made possible through the knowledge and measurement of nuclear forces, gravity, background radiation, and of course, the speed of light. The sciences of mathematics, nuclear physics, quantum mechanics, thermodynamics and others are also required, which stipulate certain laws, principles and 'absolutes' which are used in those calculations and theorems."

Xi'tau lay on his back and snored loudly. Teecha picked up a small stone, tossed it onto the lion and shouted: "*Tula*!" meaning 'quiet!' in the Zulu language. The muscles on Xi'tau's back twitched, he swished his tail, stood up and stretched. Turning round twice, he flopped down again and laying his big head on his forepaws, stared disapprovingly at us for a few seconds.

I lit another cigarette and asked: “You speak Zulu too?”

Teecha complained: “Ace, you smoke too much.”

I laughed it off and queried: “Teecha, surely if the age of the universe could be determined then it must have had a beginning – like earth. That’s logical, isn’t it?” “Logic is something one uses to arrive at conclusions when you think you know all the facts. It works, but you seldom have all the facts – ask any woman.”

“Now that’s logic,” I remarked laughingly. Teecha’s face wrinkled up in a smile but quickly turned serious again. “Women use intuition more than men, Ace. And intuition is a fact that often triumphs over all others. To disregard intuition is the way of a fool.”

My smile disappeared.

“Those laws and absolutes I mentioned are the precise reasons preventing scientists from explaining a beginning. By going backwards in time, theoretically, certain models of an infant universe may be constructed, even to the last split second before ‘the beginning’. If a beginning can be explained, then at that instant, time has to begin as well. In other words, time must then be zero. One of the absolutes in thermodynamics is absolute zero temperature, at minus 273 degrees Celsius or 0 degrees Kelvin. Present knowledge suggests that nothing could get colder than that.

“Another absolute is termed Planck’s wall, which is basically the highest temperature that matter (or energy) could achieve after which it just cannot exist in any known form. Planck’s wall can never be crossed, as matter or energy can never be destroyed. Most models of an early universe, moving back to when time was supposedly zero, suggest that the temperature of matter or whatever energy forces could create matter, gets higher and higher the closer it gets to the ‘beginning’. Planck’s wall comes before time can be zero, at around 10 to the power of minus 43 of a second. That is indeed a split second, but enough to nullify all efforts to explain a beginning.”

I interrupted once more: “Teecha, that is as close to BANG! as you can get – isn't that enough proof that there was a beginning?"

He continued with just a glance in my direction:

"Stephan Hawking, one of this century's greatest scientists and cosmologists and likened to another Einstein, spends most of his life trying to find an explanation for the beginning. He says:

'The Planck wall is the universe's ultimatum: there will be no further hedging of equations, no more jumping over points too complex to understand. This is where all your calculations and all your thinking must be brought together in the clearest statement in the history of mankind about the cosmos before you will know how it began. And still you may never know – exactly.'

"In reality Ace, you do not have to rule out any of the beliefs or theories I mentioned, for the simple reason that creation is still continuing and 'big bangs' are happening all over the universe right now. You still have many things to discover and to rediscover. Those may change your beliefs and scientific laws once again, but I want you to consider the following: There was NO beginning!"

Teecha paused as he obviously knew the impact of his words. For a moment I thought he was having me on but quickly realized he was deadly serious.

I considered his statement thoroughly and then replied: "That's difficult to fathom... No Teecha, what you say is total hogwash – there must have been a beginning!"

"Ace, you're the one who asks the questions and who talks about logic. Now open your mind to a few facts, intuition and a little reasoning."

He had a point so I decided to hear him out.

"All of us can distinguish between 'something' and 'nothing' – that is quite easy. You either have something, let's say in your hands, or you have nothing. If you have something in your hands, it consists of some form of matter, like a stone or book or your smoking cigarette. Matter consists of particles like protons, electrons and neutrons. These particles combine in many different ways to form atoms. The fact is, matter is something that can be seen, touched, smelled, tasted or heard. You hear things because of sound waves traveling through matter, like through the clean air we're breathing right now.

"Matter also exists and can be sensed in many other forms, for example energy, which could be classified into things such as fire, heat and light. Fire for instance, is a form of matter that man rediscovered and termed 'plasm'. 'Rediscovered' in the sense that ancient cultures on Earth knew that all matter exists in four basic forms, which they termed 'earth', 'water', 'air' and 'fire'. Today, you too know that matter exists in only four forms, that of solids, liquids, gases and energy (plasm). Energy, which itself exists in many different forms, can be transformed back into any other form of matter or it can be stored as potential or chemical energy.

"By the way Ace, the word 'plasm' means a mold or matrix in which anything is cast or formed: There is infinite energy or plasm in the universe, thus anything is possible..."

It was getting chilly. Teecha shifted his crossed legs and threw more wood onto the fire. He remained silent and I tried to absorb what he had said, especially his last comment. It made some sense but I decided to question it anyway: "Teecha, how do you know there is infinite energy?"

He scratched his gray hair and still remained silent. I thought that this time I had caught him out and waited expectantly. When he answered though, I realized that he was only thinking about the best way to explain it to me.

"The law of conservation of energy states that the total energy of the universe is constant. That is consistent with the theory of relativity as proposed by one of your greatest scientists. Plants transform and store sunlight into chemical energy through a process called photosynthesis, which man has not yet been able to copy from nature. Our campfire for instance, destroys wood to coals and ashes, releasing stored chemical energy in the wood as light and heat. That light or heat could be used by some other process to transform it into yet another form of matter. Energy can never be destroyed nor created.

"If you believe in God like you told me you do, then you should know this, as God was never created... Anyway, the fact that energy, which is matter, cannot be destroyed but only transformed from one form into another, means that the quantity of matter existing throughout the universe is absolute: it can not be added to or made less. And on the other hand, matter is also infinite, meaning there is no measure to it. Bear this in mind..."

My mind was already bearing enough, at the same trying to pre-empt what Teecha meant with his statement about 'no beginning'. By then I realized that he was not going to be sidetracked and that he would make his point in his own time. I tried to speed him up anyway: "Teecha, what you're saying is certainly possible but I still can't see why there was no beginning, and what did you mean with..."

His upheld hand stopped me right there: "OK Ace, OK... The opposite to matter (something) is simply nothing. In no uncertain terms the word 'nothing' means just what it implies: 'no-thing', absolutely no matter – not a single atom, not heat, not light but a complete void or vacuum. In this hi-tech age of yours you use many appliances or other machinery operating under the principle of a vacuum. Do you possess a vacuum-cleaner or are you familiar with the fact that your vehicle's power-brakes work under the same law?"

I nodded.

"Do you know that every time you breathe your chest and diaphragm muscles create a partial vacuum inside your lungs, which sucks air, which is matter, into your lungs?"

I nodded again and he continued questioning:

"So what do you need to create a vacuum with, Ace? What do you need to create a space, of any size, in which this vacuum or 'nothing' could exist? Think about it – all you have to do is to set aside some space, let's say one cubic meter, in which there is absolutely nothing, in other words an absolute void... What would you need to do just that?" My mind searched for something but again he answered his own questions without giving me a chance:

"Eheh, Ace, most people's logic would reason that you would need a container or 'something' of that nature from which you could suck out all the air or whatever is inside it to create the vacuum. How else would you do it, Ace?"

He seemed very sure that there was no other way. Neither could I come up with an alternative. I shrugged my shoulders and said: "No idea."

"Now then, let's see what we've figured out so far: Firstly, you need SOME-thing to confine this NO-thing in. Secondly, you need to suck out or disperse whatever matter there is inside some container to create the vacuum. To do that you will need energy of some kind, which is just matter in another form, and you will have your 'NO-thing'... By now Ace, you should understand just what I'm telling you – that there was no beginning!"

He still didn't make sense to me and the blank expression in my eyes must have made that quite clear. He looked at me expectantly though, waiting for something to dawn upon my face but it never happened. He threw both hands into the air, looked up to the heavens for support and gave a desperate sigh: "You're a difficult one," he mumbled. Then, as if groping for the last straw, he said: "What I've just told you is that '*nothing*' cannot exist without '*something*': You cannot have a vacuum unless you have a container, consisting of matter, in which the vacuum can exist. What would you need if you want to make your 'nothing' incredibly big or even an infinite size?"

As if I wasn't there he answered his own question once more: "You'd need 'something' of an incredible or infinite size as well. Why then, do you have this problem with something being created out of nothing? Why do people want to prove a beginning which never was? That is senseless, Ace – the universe exists as matter, which is 'something', and as space, which is 'nothing'..."

At that stage he must have sensed a faint flicker of comprehension from the depths of my mind. Looking relieved that his efforts were not wasted, he continued seriously: "In the true sense, outer space is not a complete vacuum as it is full of particles like photons and the like. These particles in space, compared to solid bodies of matter like suns and planets, are sufficiently scarcely distributed that for practical purposes, space could be considered a vacuum. Think about this, Ace: If you can imagine the universe to end somewhere, then what will it be that ends it? It could, if that was the case, only be 'something', and if something does end it, then where does that something end? More 'nothing' after that, and then? Consider it the other way around: If our universe consisted entirely as a solid block of 'something', then what and where would that end? And if that something does end somewhere, with nothing after that, then where and what will end the nothing?"

Teecha obviously knew that he had hit the target. I had neither an answer nor another question to ask. Deep in thought, I had trouble concentrating on what he said next: "Quite simply Ace, 'nothing' cannot exist without 'something', and the opposite of that, being that something cannot exist without nothing, is equally true. Baruch Spinoza, a 17th century Dutch philosopher, speculated that infinity could be either finite or infinite. By 'finite' infinity he meant something which has no end in its own kind – thus matter, he believed, can only be limited by more matter, which means that matter is infinite. The same could be said about space, thus space is infinite. The universe, and there is only ONE universe, is nothing more than these two opposites, matter and space, eternally coexisting within eternity..."

He didn't have to say anything more. I realized for the first time in my life that we all know what the word 'eternity' means. We frequently use it in our everyday conversations but seldom think that what we really say, is that there was no beginning, and that there will never be an End.

"Eheh, Teecha, '*Dis maar net so*'"...

******

"Whatever is has already been,
and what will be
has been before..."

(Ecclesiastes 3:15)

THE SECOND DAY

Standing up from next to the campfire, Teecha said: “Tomorrow is another day, Ace; Sleep well.”

I wished him a good night too. He walked over to where Xi’tau was lying and lay down next to him.

That night it was me who sat motionless with my thoughts, just staring into the dying coals. I tried to figure out what was happening to me, why I was there and whether I was still thinking rationally. How was it possible for a Bushman to know all the things he told me and why did he do it? Sure enough, I’d asked him to but right then it seemed absurd. Utterly confusing, in fact. Something told me that Teecha had much more to tell. His reply earlier that night about who he was or could be also bothered me. Was he really a Bushman?

Curiosity made up my mind and I decided to spend one more day with him. My water supply should last and I consoled myself that the family back home was used to expecting me a day or two late after excursions into the bush.

Looking silently at the frail human body next to a lion three or more times his size, confused me even more. They were both fast asleep – at least it looked that way, though I wasn’t too sure about my own concept of reality. I picked up a small stone, thought twice about what I intended doing, and then did it anyway – I flicked it onto Xi’tau. My pulse raced as the skin on his back twitched, his eyes slowly opened and he stared at me disgustedly. I could have sworn that I heard: “Now what did you do that for?”

With shaking hands I added more wood to the fire but when I guiltily glanced at the lion again his eyes were closed. “There must be a lot more to this,” I concluded and decided to turn in too. Although I was physically tired, I had a restless night. Unwilling to succumb to sleep, my mind tried to make sense of Teecha’s words. Time and again I found myself outside the sleeping bag, shivering in the cold.

Wide-awake yet again, I peeped outside. The fire had long since burnt out and clouds covered the stars. The pitch-blackness of the night was gloomy. Wondering what time it was, I fumbled in the dark for the torch and switched it on, but then remembered that I had left my watch inside the vehicle. "So what – to heck with it. Get some sleep." It must have been close to 3am. I switched the torch off and darkness ensued. On impulse, I switched it back on. "Magic," I thought, "now you see, now you don't."

Like a child I kept switching the torch on and off, wondering about this thing called light. Recalling Teecha's words that tomorrow was another day, I realized that very soon a big and brilliant light would be turned on, announcing just that. A scops owl hooted nearby and, still wondering about light, I finally fell into a deep sleep. The sun must have been up for more than an hour when I woke, my eyes straining to grow accustomed to the brightness outside.

Teecha offered me coffee.

"Thanks," I mumbled. "Did you sleep well?"

He made no comment and feeling embarrassed for sleeping so late I explained: "Your words kept me up all night."

"Eheh, so I noticed. Did you have a problem getting your torch to switch off?"

I wondered if he ever slept! "I was thinking about light," I explained. "– it's a wonderful thing."

"Eheh, you missed the best part at sunrise."

I was still searching for an appropriate comment when he said, smiling: "Let's find breakfast."

Taking my usual few things, we set off. Teecha seemed to know where he was going, for he kept moving northwest. Half an hour later we came upon a tall monkey orange tree full of ripe fruit. He climbed the tree and picked a few of the orange-like fruits, throwing them down for me to catch. They had a hard wooden shell, which had to be cracked open against a stone. Inside was a delicious custard-yellow flesh with a sort of sweet 'n' sour taste. I put a few in my rucksack, deciding to plant and grow the seeds back home.

As we walked further, I discovered more and more edible plants: One could eat either their fruits, bulbs, tubers, roots or berries. At one stage, Teecha started picking the leaves from a patch of weeds. "This is wild spinach, Ace. We call it '*merogo*'. Pick the young leaves only."

Other edible plants showed two or three tiny leaves above the ground, hiding a large juicy bulb underneath which could be pulped into a thirst quenching drink. Wild raisins were rather tasty and I soon learned to grab a handful whenever we passed some bushes with ripe ones growing. *Tsama* melons lay around here and there and Teecha prepared a fruit cocktail inside the shell of one, by mixing it with the sweeter monkey-orange flesh. It was still slightly bitter but certainly drinkable. In times of drought *tsama* melons are a source of water, not only for antelope and many other animals, but also for the Bushman people.

Around noon we found more mushrooms and my mouth started watering. I was considering frying them on the coals like Teecha had done when I thought about something I had always wanted to see and asked him: "Can you make fire?"

He knew that I carried my cigarette lighter but understood what I meant immediately. "Eheh... I'll show you how."

He searched for what he needed as I watched in expectation. After finding two pieces of wood that I could tell from his smile were obviously suitable, together with a handful of soft dry grass and leaves from a resin bush, he asked for my knife. One piece of wood was a stick about 40cm (16 inches) long and slightly thicker than a pencil, the other just a splinter of rather hard and heavy wood, about 20 cm (eight inches) long and 5cm (two inches) thick. Into this he made a small hollow with the knife, then rounded one end of the longer piece to fit snugly into it.

Sitting cross-legged he pinned the thick piece down with his feet and inserted the end of the other into the hollow. He then started twirling the long piece by rubbing it between his hands, which moved swiftly up and down the stick as he applied pressure to its end. After a few minutes the friction between the two pieces of wood produced more smoke than my cigarette, at which stage Teecha inspected the end of one piece briefly. Not satisfied with the result he continued again. After another minute or so, he quickly added grass and leaves to the point of friction and still twirling vigorously, blew gently onto the kindling. A fair amount of smoke rose from his 'lighter'. It wasn't too long before a flame appeared. He quickly added more grass, leaves and twigs. Out of sheer appreciation for his effort I clapped my hands and shouted: "Fire! fire!" He grinned.

The fried mushrooms went down well, without butter. Neither of us were hungry that evening but finding a packet of long-life cream (reserved for Irish coffee), I prepared creamed wild spinach for a snack. We literally licked our bowls clean while chatting about the day's experiences. I made a few notes of the plants he showed me for further study and wondered whether I would find the details in some textbook. I also wondered if I would be able to get a fire going like he did – it looked so easy. Watching the flames of our campfire casting light all around, reminded me of my episode with the torch the previous night.

"Light is fantastic," I remarked. Not in the least prepared for what followed, I asked: "Teecha, what do you know about light?"

That evening I realized there was more to our meeting than coincidence. Teecha was a maestro of life and knowledge from whom I just had to learn more. I really had no choice but to stay another day... maybe two.

******

LIGHT

"Only if we know that
the thing that truly matters
is the infinite
can we avoid fixing our interest
upon futilities"

Carl Gustav Jung, 'Memories, Dreams, Reflections'

"Light is the lifeblood of eternity, Ace..."

At first it seemed as if he considered his explanation good enough. After a while though, I realized something and said: "OK Teecha, you have a way of getting me to think – now what do you mean with that?"

"I have many things to tell you. It is good that you ask me about light because if you don't know what it is, nothing else will make much sense. You're searching for the meaning of life and you'll only find it through light. It'll be easier if you know what it is."

When he paused, I questioned skeptically: "Teecha, light is an interesting phenomenon but I don't see the connection. What has light got to do with the search for meaning in life?"

"Everything."

His reply didn't make any sense and I repeated: "Everything? Why?"

"Light is matter which is; without it there is nothing but 'the Nothing'."

He certainly had a way to excite my gray matter. "OK, I'm listening."

"Only during the last few decades, so you believe, did man begin to understand what light really is. Apart from its physical features, it is the basic requirement of all life forms. Without light in the many forms it exists, there is no life. On earth there are many life forms spending their whole life underground or in the darkest of caves. However, they would never have evolved and survived if it were not for light supplying heat inside their places of confined existence. To you they live in total darkness but those species lost the need for sight or never required it – they have other highly developed senses. Others again, see perfectly well where you humans cannot even **see** the light at the end of the tunnel, because you yourselves switch it off from time to time."

I smiled. "Yes, I suppose we often do that, but how come they can see what we don't?"

"Like with so many other things, humans see a very small part of the light spectrum. You call those light-rays which your eyes sense 'visible light'. Other life forms sense or see different parts of the light spectrum, as your own body does: an overdose of ultraviolet or infrared rays causes sunburn, usually accompanied by extreme pain. Many other forms of light exist, like X-rays and radio waves. Radio and television programs are transmitted to your ears or eyes using light as the basic principle. You transmit light, sometimes via satellite, from one part of your globe and receive it at another, where your clever TV boxes change that light back into a visible and audible form."

I interrupted: "Teecha, you're really something else, but yes, I know about the things you're telling me. The fact is, there is light. What I wanted to know is: Why?"

He stared at me strangely for a few seconds, then uttered that weird '*Tchi... tchi...*' sound before challenging me.

"You want to know 'why?' – then why don't you listen?"

I made a helpless gesture and decided to do just that.

He took his time before continuing, factually: "Right, you accepted that matter exists and that space exists. Mankind studied matter for years and has discovered many of its secrets and characteristics. You know that it consists of a number of 'particles', of which you have identified more than 40 to date. These particles combine to form atoms, which make up more than a hundred different elements – the pure forms of matter such as neon, oxygen, mercury, silver or gold. The atoms of these different elements can combine with each other in an unthinkable number of combinations to form molecules, in which form most organic (related to life) and inorganic (inanimate) substances exist."

Although at the time I knew most of the things Teecha told me, I found it fascinating just listening to him. He was absolutely serious and explained everything he said with all sorts of gestures and expressions. It was rather difficult to keep my pose through it all, but somehow I managed. Where at first I found his knowledge unacceptable, coming from a Bushman, I slowly shifted that feeling to the back of my mind and made peace with it. However, that peace didn't last very long.

"Nature provides hundreds of molecular substances and man continually discovers or manufactures more. You have learned how to use the basic building block of matter, the atom, to your advantage – and to your detriment. You can split the atom and release inconceivable energies. Hydrogen bombs and nuclear power stations are enough evidence of man's knowledge concerning matter. However, your control of that knowledge is primitive: Hiroshima and Chernobyl are just two cases."

He surely had a way of keeping my attention and knew how to upset me. "Everybody makes mistakes, Teecha – it's the only way to learn."

"Aowa, Ace, that's rubbish!" he exclaimed, "Once you have that kind of knowledge, you're not allowed any mistakes! And you don't have to learn through mistakes – there are easier ways."

I certainly didn't expect such a reaction to my simple statement.

"OK," I said, "calm down – you know what I mean."

He said, almost scolding: "Eheh, but you don't!"

This time I felt anger rising but managed to control it. I said coldly: "Teecha, please get to the point."

As if I was a stubborn kid, he slowly shook his head from side to side and sound-clicked that *"Tchi, tchi..."* thing of his once again. I was about to get up for some fresh air when he continued.

"Ace, before considering some basic laws of matter, I want to tell you a few things about the particles which make up atoms. We don't have to delve into complex physics, but these particles are of particular interest.

Each has either a positive or negative charge, hence the terms 'matter' for positively charged particles, and 'antimatter' for negatively charged particles. The term antimatter doesn't mean something that does not exist – in fact, both matter and antimatter have mass (weight) unless it exists in the form of energy. There seems to be a required balance between positive and negative particles in every atom. If this is not the case, then an imbalanced particle will spontaneously change into another form of existence, or join up with another lonely particle of the opposite charge – if it finds such a mate."

A thought flashed through my mind. "Wait!" I said and held up my hand: "Teecha, in nature there are organisms where a female changes into a male or vice versa when there is an imbalance of partners. Are you telling me that this happens even at subatomic levels, to maintain some kind of balance?"

He calmly told me: "Eheh, that's where it starts and ends Ace. There is an ultimate balance, called 'yin' and 'yang' – female and male if you take it back to basics. And remember that all the ancient scripts mention yin, the female, first. But you're jumping the gun."

I opened my mouth to say something but he must have decided it was going to be irrelevant. He continued as if I didn't exist:

"When particles are forced to exist on their own, they quickly 'decay' into something else, some existing in their new form for a split second only. For example, when electrons are energized, in other words forced to become imbalanced, they emit or absorb 'photons' to maintain the positive/negative balance. Photons are mass-less particles, which exist as electromagnetic energy such as common light waves, heat waves or radio waves. All photons move rather fast. To date they are the fastest things in the universe you know about. Light is nothing but a stream of photon particles, which is matter, thus it IS.

"And now Ace, how about coffee?"

I thought he wasn't going to say anything more. A little disappointed, I agreed: "Good idea," and got up to fill the kettle. He still hadn't answered my question, though. I started up again. "Teecha, that was fascinating stuff but..." when he completed my sentence: "But you still don't know why, right Ace?"

I spilled the water and stuttered: "Yes, ahh... No... How the heck do you know what I'm thinking?"

"Coffee first."

I made it in silence and handed him a mug. He nodded thanks and while blowing it cold, sipped loudly but slowly. Watching him until he put his mug down, I forgot to drink mine. He continued as if there had been no break.

"There are many other particles known to exist and your scientists discover more all the time. They are classified as elementary and resonance particles. These subatomic little things have collectively been grouped as 'quarks' and are subdivided into 'baryons', 'mesons', 'leptons', 'hyperons' and others. But enough of that – let's leave them to your nuclear physicists. There is one characteristic or law of matter however, which is of great importance:

'Matter attracts matter in whatever form it exists'.

"This fundamental law of the behavior of matter was discovered by Isaac Newton, to whom you owe a lot of your present understanding of gravity and the reasons why you do not fall off the earth. According to legend, Newton was resting under an apple tree, when one of the fruits fell on his head. That unexpected 'conk', with impact in relation to the height of the apple from his brain, probably caused him to discuss Granny Smith, but it also assisted him in formulating the Newtonian laws. They govern the fact that the earth stays in orbit around the sun, the moon stays in its orbit around you, and your solar system stays in this galaxy.

"Since the days of Newton, man discovered more fundamental laws acting on matter. The law that caused the apple to fall on Newton's head, called gravity, acts on and controls the largest objects in the universe. It is by far, though, the weakest of four forces that influence the behavior of all matter. The strongest forces operate on particles at subatomic levels.

The strongest of the four, aptly called 'the strong nuclear force', holds the nucleus of an atom together. The second strongest force, called electro-magnetism, keeps electrons in orbit around the nucleus of an atom, allowing matter to exist in normal states as most elements do at normal temperatures. The third force, called 'the weak force', causes radioactive decay in elements like uranium. The fourth force is gravity, extremely weak in comparison to the others. But note Ace, that the strongest physical force in the universe acts on the smallest objects while the weakest force, but no means the least, controls the largest."

I wanted to ask him about these forces but decided to remain silent and see what happened. He didn't let me down.

"Today, man knows what some of these forces are, while others still defy explanation. For instance, you know exactly what is responsible for the three stronger forces acting on all matter, being transmitted by particles called 'vector bosons'. Bosons exist for a fraction of a second, during which time they transmit their attracting force to and fro between the particles, which combine to form an atom. A boson called a 'gluon' accounts for the strong nuclear force. The photon particle (light) causes electromagnetism while 'W' and 'Z' particles cause radioactivity."

This thing that he appeared to read my thoughts was disturbing and I tried to discard it as mere chance. Teecha carried on, seemingly unaware of my concern:

"Speculation is that a 'graviton' is responsible for the fourth force, but man has no proof that it exists. The thing you're worrying about right now Ace, may be transmitted by a particle termed an 'imagon'."

"What!" I exclaimed and sat up straight: "You mean to say thought?"
"Eheh, that accounts for things like telepathy and other Extra Sensory Perceptions, if you can 'imagon' that, but that's beside the point."

I opened my mouth to say something but my voice had gone.

"'Nothing' is the only impossible thing, Ace – everything else is."

Leaning back on my chair I wished to be thoughtless too.

"Now you're thinking like a *Mamparra*," he remarked.

In native folklore, a Mamparra is a silly, mindless creature, like a moron. I remained speechless.

"You know that particles of opposite charge attract one another and then become or behave reasonably stable. Now, what would happen if many chunks of matter were to float around in outer space, or in other words, if there were lots of something within lots of nothing?"

He answered himself again: "Of course, they will be attracted together though they may be parsecs apart, like moths and even humans are attracted to a source of light. If we assume that these pieces of matter could be of any size, just a particle or a monstrous mass, then at some stage they'll meet. In fact, they'll physically collide, because the gravitational force attracting them in the first place also causes them to accelerate towards each other. You have already observed and catalogued other galaxies that have collided and for all you know, your own is on its way to meet another – it is certainly moving fast enough.

"Now how did all this motion come about? Ace. Ever seen an explosion of reasonable size, with objects flying and spinning through the air?" He jerked me back to reality and I was reminded of army days behind the gunner's sight in a modern tank.

"Now imagine something similar but on a massive scale. Imagine the energies involved in the explosions that created your galaxy. If you can, then you have your answer."

Scenes of exploding bombs flashed through my mind, wreaking havoc and destruction. They faded and were replaced by a blinding light, which turned into a devastating mushroom, but I obviously didn't use my imagination properly.

"Aowa, you'll have to do much better than that!"

It was getting late. I was cold, the night dark, and the Kalahari quiet.

"That's better, Ace!" Teecha said, "let's take it from there."

I looked at him totally puzzled but his eyes were closed and he murmured softly...

******

“We are somewhere in outer space, millions of light years from your home planet, Earth. Time is of no concern – we’re in Eternity. There is only silence, it is bitterly cold and the darkness around us is so black that we can almost feel it. We are spirits with no material form. Neither cold nor heat affect us. We’re in a theatre called ‘The Universe’, watching the drama of ‘Creation’ which is unfolding before us on the Stage of Life. We sense lots of matter around us, primarily consisting of hydrogen and helium gases – it’s all over the place. The atmosphere is tense in anticipation. Then a loud voice says the words:

‘Let there be light...’

Act 1:

ALPHA

Gravitation slowly pulls the atoms of these gases together over millions of years, to form a huge cloud of gas, maybe a hundred or more light years across. Knowing what it can do, gravitation continues to exert its relentless force, causing the central parts of the gas cloud to compress even more, which in turn causes a greater pull on the outer layers of the cloud. It slowly starts to ‘collapse’ inward upon itself.

Once this collapse begins, nothing can stop this fatal attraction of matter to matter; the cloud gets smaller and smaller and its density becomes higher and higher. As the central density increases, the gravitational pull becomes stronger and stronger and the collapse continues more rapidly. This causes friction, which heats up the matter to a temperature of millions of degrees. This tremendous energy, in turn, eventually provides sufficient pressure to halt the collapse, transforming the initial cloud of matter into an incredibly hot sphere of gas, shining brightly – a star is born!

... ‘and there was light’...

Act 2:

LIBRA

After the whole commotion with all that matter, pieces of very hot debris are also floating around. Many different forces act upon the inertia of these moving objects, which eventually cool down and become planets, moons, comets and asteroids, firmly balancing them in specific orbits around each other and their sun.

Let's see, however, what fate has in mind for our newborn star.

For many millions of years after its creation, it keeps on shining brightly. Through some Universal Force, life evolves on one or more of its planets, over many eons. Unaware of this, our star supports life in many different forms, over many different times. All the time the intense heat in its interior provides enough pressure to counteract the inward gravitational pull of the matter it consists of.

Heat and light are continuously being lost from the surface, but replenished through thermonuclear reactions: lighter atoms, such as the hydrogen gas that originally formed the star, are being 'fused' into heavier atoms. This process releases tremendous energies in the form of heat and light – like never ending hydrogen bomb explosions lashing out tens of thousands of kilometers from the surface...

Act 3:

OMEGA

After billions of years, our star's supply of nuclear fuel runs out so that it can no longer replenish the energy radiating away from it. When this happens, it also loses its thermal pressure, allowing that fatal attraction of matter for matter to take over: 'Death' stares it in the face.

Depending on our star's original size, its certain death may happen in a number of different ways. If its size was roughly that of the one in your own solar system, it would die a relatively peaceful death: gravity keeps pulling it inward upon itself, but eventually, any further compression provides sufficient pressure to halt the inward collapse, and although it continues to shine weakly for a few more million years, it is essentially dead. There are a few stars in this phase that you know about and they are called 'white dwarfs'.

However, our star's ultimate fate is certain. Cooling down further, it will become nothing but a cold, dark chunk of matter once more, floating endlessly through space. But gravity waits in the void, patiently..."

******

"Ace," Teecha called and rudely shocked me back to Earth, "as a matter of interest, the first of these white dwarfs to be discovered was the companion of the brightest star in your heavens, namely Sirius, in the constellation Canis Major. Sirius is known as 'The Dog Star', accompanying Orion, 'The Hunter'. The white dwarf close to Sirius is now called Sirius 'B', which can only be seen with powerful radio telescopes. What makes Sirius B interesting is that there is a tribe of people in Africa called the Dojos, who claim their ancestors came from that star. The Dojos had pointed to the bright Sirius many years ago, before the discovery of Sirius B and said: "That is where our ancestors came from – not from the bright star you see, but from the one close to it, which you cannot see..."

It rang a bell somewhere and I said: "Yes, I've heard about it but apparently their allegation was disproved."

Teecha replied: "Where there is smoke there is fire. Why would a so-called 'primitive' tribe build their villages in patterns representing the constellation and orbits of celestial objects, and why would they fake a tale like that?"

Something else was on my mind, though, and I asked him:

"You mentioned other ways a star can die. Like how?"

He stood up and stretched his legs. Xi'tau did the same and stared at him expectantly. "*Robala*," Teecha commanded and the lion lay down again, satisfied that his master was not leaving. 'Robala' means 'go to sleep'. "It's late Ace, but I'll tell you." He sat down again and poked the fire.

"You may just be fortunate that your sun is a star of less than normal size, classified as a 'yellow dwarf,' with a diameter of only one million three hundred and eighty three thousand and forty kilometers. A star about one and a half times bigger than your own has to face another death. After exhausting its energy, its mere size and hence the inward gravitational pull overrides any thermal pressure and it is pulled into itself in a catastrophic collapse – similar to its creation but much more violent – maybe within a few minutes.

"This 'sudden death' may come about in two ways. If it wasn't too big (less than five times the size of your sun), the collapse would come to a grinding halt, caused by nuclear repulsion. At the onset, the star's diameter may have been millions of kilometers, while at this stage it may only be about twenty kilometers. When the collapse is halted, energy is released in hundreds of millions of degrees, sufficient to blast off the outer layers of the star in a massive explosion. It suddenly becomes brighter than millions of suns together, and is called a 'super nova'."

Even as I decided to ask, he answered with just a touch of grumpiness:

"Eheh, there **is** proof of that. One of them was discovered on 19 February 1987, when astronomers detected a super nova explosion, which happened in the Large Magellanic star cloud, situated in one of the spiral arms of your own galaxy. It happened more than 160,000 light years ago, as that was the time it took the light of that cosmic death to reach Earth. It could be seen for several months with the aid of your modern radio telescopes. A code was given for this super nova, namely 1987A, being the first observed in 1987. Of equal interest is the fact that astronomers are now fairly certain that the Star of Bethlehem, which appeared at the birth of Christ, was exactly such a super nova, much closer to you than 1987A, so that it could clearly be seen with the naked eye..."

I was eager to here more but Teecha yawned loudly, making sure I got the message. He continued, though:

"The second way in which a giant star can die is far more dramatic. At this stage it is rather theoretical but evidence of such deaths have been detected by the Hubble telescope launched into space, and even before that. In 1973 evidence of such a star-death had been discovered in the constellation Cygnus, within the binary-star system called Cygnus X-1. This is what may happen if the star is very massive, like the red star Betelgeuse, part of the well-known Orion cluster, which is a mind-boggling three hundred million kilometers in diameter:

"The inward collapse may start as I mentioned before, but because of its mass, gravitation will be so strong that nothing could halt the collapse. In fact, gravitation will become so strong that not even light could escape that inconceivable force. All the light rays, being matter in the form of photons and thus subject to gravitation, will be pulled back into the star so that it can no longer be seen... However, this 'dead' star will continue to exert its gravitational influence, now secretly, on all other material objects nearby, and 'nearby' could mean many light-years. All of those objects will continue to react to that invisible force, for which you have conjured up the term 'a black hole'.

"A few last thoughts for you to sleep on… According to Einstein's Special Theory of Relativity, if it is possible for such a star to re-explode, it cannot do so in the same region of space-time in which it collapsed. If it does re-explode, it will suddenly gush out matter in another region of space and/or time. Man is on the right track with his postulations about 'white holes'. If your latest astronomical findings and evidence are correct, then there you appear to have it – 'something' out of 'nothing', which should not be too difficult for you to fathom, as both that something and that nothing existed before...

"It's time for bed Ace, but think about this:

Time within eternity has no meaning – creation of light and life happens right now and cannot ever end..."

******

‘You look out the window and you’re looking back across blackness of space a quarter of a million miles away, looking back at the most beautiful star in the heavens. You’re not close enough to any other planets to see anything but a bright star, but you can look back on Earth and see from pole to pole and across oceans and continents, and you can watch it turn and see there are no strings holding it up, and it’s moving in a blackness almost beyond conception.

The Earth is surrounded by blackness though you’re looking through sunlight. There is only light if the sunlight has something to shine on. When the sun shines through space, it’s black. All because the light doesn’t strike anything, so all you see is black.

What are you looking at? What are you looking through? You can call it the universe, but it’s the infinity of space and the infinity of time.’

Eugene Cernan (USA Astronaut) from ‘*The Home Planet*’, by K Kelly

THE THIRD DAY

Around noon we returned to our camp from an interesting morning in the bush. Apart from what Teecha had told me the previous day, he was a walking encyclopedia of knowledge on plants, insects, birds and other animals. Tired, hot and relieved to sit down, I made a few notes of the things he had told me and showed me. The midday temperature bordered around 30 degrees Celsius, average for the autumn / fall season in the Kalahari. There wasn't a cloud in sight and the sun scorched down, causing all life to enjoy a siesta, except for the sun beetles. I felt sweaty and sticky and was tempted to use some of my last water for a solar heated shower that evening.

"No go," I warned myself – there was barely enough drinking water for the next day or two. I lazily fiddled with a few things, did the washing up in a small bowl and then sat down to sharpen my knife. Teecha wanted to use the sharpening stone as well and started to sharpen his spears meticulously. After a while, true to form, he unexpectedly remarked:

"If you feel like a shower, why don't you use sand?"

"Sand? Are you serious?"

"Eheh, just dig a few inches into the moist sand and then rub it over your body – you'll be surprised. And you won't waste water." He gestured towards the shade of the umbrella thorn. The thought of having a sand-bath had never occurred to me before, but by then I had learned not to question his ideas too quickly. Without fuss, I took a spade and started digging in the sand underneath the big acacia. Sure enough, a few inches down it was damp. Removing my boots, I stuck my feet into it and was reminded of a television advert – 'Good and clean and fresh'. Next my shirt came off and my pants soon after. Rubbing my body with moist sand, which dried quickly in the heat, I just had to dust myself to feel cool and refreshed.

Experimenting further I tried it on my hair. At first I thought that was a terrible mistake. Soon, however, it was possible to shake and rub all the dried sand from my hair and a good brushing did the final trick. A glance in a small mirror I had fitted on the side of the vehicle told me I was ready for dinner in a posh restaurant... Well almost, for then my clothes felt dirty and I needed a shave rather badly. A dozen juicy prawns in lemon butter sauce made my mouth water. Something else bothered me though: how come Teecha managed to stay so clean? And so far he had never complained about the heat nor the cold.

"It's time for hunting," he said out of the blue.

"Hunting?..." It must've been the last thing on my mind.

"Eheh, you have little food left and Xi'tau is also hungry – he hasn't eaten for a few days. Let's go."

It was around 3pm. "Time flies," I thought, realizing that I had lost track of date and time completely. "What day was it?"

"Never mind Ace, come!"

Reading my thoughts as before, Teecha took his spears and set off into the bush. He gave a loud whistle and Xi'tau, dozing close-by underneath a buffalo thorn tree, lifted his head, snarled and flattened his ears. Slightly disturbed I scratched my head. The thought that the lion also had to eat never crossed my mind, so I got a good idea and shouted after Teecha:

"I'll be OK. You two go ahead while I finish up here!"

Silence was my answer as Xi'tau got up, staring at me. The expression on his face made everything clear: It was a much better idea to follow Teecha.

I caught up with him in a few seconds, after stumbling over a shrub and snapping a twig.

"Walk like I taught you to do Ace – we're hunting!"

Not half a kilometer from camp we came across a herd of springbok lazily grazing in the afternoon sun. They had seen us but were unconcerned, although we kept on walking openly. About 200 meters from them Teecha held up his hand and pointed to a lone ram some distance from the herd, saying softly:

"He has been thrown out of the herd and is of no use to them."

Stooping down, he picked up a handful of sand which he threw into the air. The dust drifted slowly towards us.

"Good, we are downwind." He gave a few short, low whistles and handed me one of his spears.

"Stay here," he commanded and started off in the direction of the lonely ram, at an angle of about 45 degrees.

I tried to follow him with my eyes but he disappeared so quickly amongst the scant shrubs and grass that I wondered whether the scene was real. My heart almost stopped as Xi'tau slowly stalked past me, head down and tail swishing. That lion meant business – he was hunting and ready for a kill. My throat became very dry (from the heat and dust) so I figured it best to follow Teecha's advice and stayed put.

After some fifteen minutes I suddenly saw Teecha again. He was now upwind from the prey, 50 meters on the other side of the springbok and me.

"Why would he do that? – surely the buck would smell him now."

Total silence. Then a gray loerie, also called the 'go-away bird', gave its long drawn-out call in the distance: 'Kwehhhhh... kwehhhh...' Hunters detest this bird for it always gives their game away – to the game.

"Yes, just as I thought": Alarmed, the buck looked up and stared motionless in Teecha's direction. After at least two minutes, it calmly started to graze again. No matter how I strained my eyes, there was no sign of Teecha or Xi'tau.

'Kwehh.. kwehh.. kwehhh...' came the call once more, now urgent. The springbok stiffened, jumped sideways and then stood motionless once more. This time it looked very wary and snorted constantly while staring tensely at something. The rest of the herd was restless too: They seemed confused, stamped their hooves on the ground and jumped to and fro, with the crest of hair above their buttocks fluffed white-open to raise alarm. It was obvious that they sensed danger but didn't know from where it would come. I thought that Teecha had changed his mind and was trying to hunt down one of the herd instead. A glance to the left and the lonely ram still stared in the direction where I last saw Teecha.

In the next second or two the hunt was over. Teecha appeared, spear held high in the air, about 20 to 30 meters away from the springbok.

"He's much too far away," I thought, having seen and marveled at the agility of these antelope many times. From its stance the buck effortlessly 'lifted' into the air for at least three meters while changing direction in midair. At that instant, I could almost feel its fear and surprise at the mistake it had made. Before it landed again, Xi'tau leapt up as if from nowhere and broke the antelope's neck with such power from his right forepaw that I heard the blow from where I stood. Pandemonium broke loose and the rest of the herd took flight, crashing through and jumping over bushes. They stampeded past me in complete confusion. Instinctively I ducked out of their way, but distinctly aware of flaring nostrils and eyes full of fear.

As abruptly as it started, so there was silence again. But for dust still hanging in the air nothing had happened. Not so sure of what to do, I got up and slowly walked in Teecha's direction. A few meters further and I caught sight of him – but what was he doing? Xi'tau stood about 10 meters away, while Teecha knelt over the dead animal.

"Impossible – Nobody just walks over and shares a lion's kill!"

It felt as though I was in a trance, my legs moving forward on their own accord. I could have sworn Teecha was praying...

"Now don't be stupid," I said aloud – "he's probably slitting the animal's throat or something." As I got closer, I noticed that he was indeed cutting flesh with his spear. He put some meat into his bag and slung another piece over his shoulder. Xi'tau took the rest of the buck in his jaws and as if it was weightless, carried it a few meters, slumped down and started his meal. A jackal's cry send a chill down my spine...

Teecha approached me smiling, as if nothing unusual had happened and remarked: "Tonight we'll have a feast." He had taken a piece of hind leg and the liver of the springbok. "Let's go home and get the fire going."

We walked back in silence, except for Teecha's one question on the way: "Do you now see why I don't need a bow and arrow?"

At the camp I said: "You relax, I'll prepare supper."

If I may say so, I have prepared some great meals for my safari clients (with the aid of recipe books), and then I wanted to impress that unique man, or maybe I just wanted to get him back, somehow. A beer and a packet of self-raising flour turned into oven fresh bread, baked in a small cast-iron pot. All the spices I could find and the last few tins of food helped me serve a fruit cocktail for starters, liver pate and roast leg of venison. I took out the tablecloths, cutlery and crockery reserved for fussy clients and opened a bottle of vintage wine. We had a feast in the bush.

"Compliments to the chef, Ace," Teecha said after the meal.

"My pleasure, sir – care for an Irish?"

"Eheh."

While sipping our doctored coffee, I wanted to know: "Teecha, tell me something – when you kneeled over that springbok today, what were you doing?"

"I prayed to his spirit, asking forgiveness."

"Forgiveness for what?"

"For killing him."

"But you didn't kill him, Xi'tau did – I saw it all."

He calmly replied: "Eheh, but I use Xi'tau, as he uses me. We all have to live, and in order to do so, some must die. That's what life is all about – you also enjoyed the meat, didn't you?"

"Yes, but it was only an animal."

"Animal my foot!" he exclaimed, and looked very annoyed with me.

Worried about his rapid change of mood, I asked: "Did I say something wrong?" "You certainly have many things to learn, Ace... Eheh, I **will** tell you something – about the Spirit"...

THE SPIRIT

Behold! thy Lord said
To the angels: "I am about
To create man, from sounding clay
From mud molded into shape;
When I have fashioned him
(In due proportion) and breathed
Into him of My spirit,
Fall ye down in obeisance
Unto him."
The Qur'an: Sura XV : 28-29

It is well known that Bushmen and other indigenous peoples like the Aborigines in Australia and the Indians of the rainforests, believe sincerely in the spirits of their forefathers and in the existence of many others, good or evil. Civilized people of course, don't concern themselves with things like that, nor with black cats, horoscopes, vampires or holy water. Teecha had already mentioned N!odima, the spirit of life. At last I thought he would tell me a little about Bushmen superstitions and other beliefs. Eager to get him started, I asked:

"Teecha, do you believe in spirits?"

By then I should have known it – I didn't quite get the answer expected.

"Ace, we cannot do otherwise than to accept that all things around us exist. Apart from what we easily perceive, there are other forces and energies, maybe unexplained, but real. Rene Descartes, a 17th century French mathematician and scientist is remembered for his famous maxim *'I think, therefore I am'*. You can't be thinking or listening to me right now if you don't exist and if I don't exist. It follows then, that we all accept the existence of other thinking entities: 'We think, therefore we are'. Not only is this logical, but emotionally necessary. No human can bear being alone. Like ants, you need to physically touch other living beings almost on a daily basis, or you could end up insane. Think how many times you touch other people almost every day of your life. Why do pets like to be stroked by their masters? Prisoners in solitary confinement often go mad, and loneliness drives people to suicide. Locking or chaining somebody up in such a way that he cannot touch another living being for a couple of weeks has been used as a very effective method of torture, which eventually forces such a person to part with secrets or to succumb to his captors."

I interrupted impatiently. "Yes, that's all true Teecha, but you're talking about physical beings; I asked if you believe in spirits."

He stared at me with a funny expression. When he uttered that strange '*Tchi.. tchi..*' sound and I sensed a shade of irritation. He continued:

"In recent tests, it was proved that seedlings grow stronger and faster if they are touched and stroked by humans every day. You probably did those experiments because you wouldn't believe the writings of a very old book, *The Royal Path of Life*, in which is said: 'Everybody knows that if you gently shake a young tree daily, it grows much faster'. But to answer your question Ace, let's call other thinking entities simply more *I's*. Now look around you... How many *I's* do you see, hear or sense?"

The night was quiet yet when I listened carefully, it wasn't. The sounds of many different insects, the scurrying of small mice, the soft rustling of dry leaves and the far-off cry of a bush baby all blended together like a kind of 'white noise'. If one didn't consciously listen, there was only silence. An unfortunate moth dive-bombed into the fire and was cremated. There were indeed many thinking entities, but I had my doubts with the moth.

Teecha broke the silence. "And what about the umbrella thorn?... Anyway, should you deny there are many other *I's* around you, then you have to deny your own existence, as none of you can exist alone – not even a plant. To accept the existence of *I's* you can perceive is easy. It is difficult though to accept that there are *I's* which you cannot perceive with your normal senses – those senses that you were taught you have. Going back to Descartes's dictum, you can change the words around to make it say: ***'I am, therefore I think'***. If you are, you think, which implies at least some ability to reason, therefore you exist."

Those last few days had given me enough reasons to worry about my reasoning ability and whether I really 'was' but Teecha didn't give me much time to think it over.

"A little more reason Ace, is all you require to show that *I's* do not all exist at the same level of consciousness, intelligence or morality. Certainly you yourself, your own I, exists on a different level than that of your dog or cat? In anthropology the zoological term for modern man is Homo sapiens, which means 'wise man'. You would be totally foolish though, to believe that mankind are the only wise beings, considering that Earth is an insignificant little planet in a remote corner between billions of stars in your own galaxy."

I had science on my side here. I replied: "That may be so, but it was calculated using our modern computers that the probability of life on another planet like Earth is 1 against 10 to the power of 30. That leaves just about no chance for any other intelligent beings like man."

Teecha scratched his head while doing his '*Tchi.. tchi..*' thing. I felt as if I had made a good move in chess.

"Ace, if you accept that, you limit *Gao!na*, not so?"

I had just lost my queen and with that the game, as he continued:

"Even with your clever computer's calculations, it leaves an infinite number of possibilities for life anywhere else: Compare that probability to eternity, which is infinity, and you'll find there are infinite chances for life as you know it, rather than no chance."

He was right of course. To refresh my memory, I scratched a simple mathematical formula for calculating probabilities on the sand. My clever move turned out to be silly. At least I felt like saying: "Now I'm getting it."

Teecha continued: "Beings of much higher intelligence and planes of consciousness certainly exist. In the Bible, 1 Corinthians 15:40 it is written: '*There are also heavenly bodies and there are earthly bodies; but the splendor of the heavenly bodies is one kind, and the splendor of the earthly bodies is another.*'

"'Extraterrestrials' as you call them in science fiction, are not fiction. You all talk about gods, angels, devils and the like. Your minds, your histories, myths and scriptures are full of them. Most of your religions are based on the existence of a Supreme Being or beings who control everything. The truth is these super beings, '*Ultraterrestials*' or 'Infinite Intelligence', simply exist as other *I's*. It may be inconceivable, but that is the case. Consider another extract from the Bible, Genesis 6 verse 4: '*The Nephilim (giants) were on the earth in those days – and also afterwards – when the sons of God went to the daughters of men and had children by them. They were the heroes of old, men of renown*'..." Teecha paused. I had become used to his way of getting me to think so I said: "Makes one think, doesn't it?"

He nodded. "OK Ace, replace '*I*' with the word 'Spirit'. This will mean that many spirits exist on different levels of intelligence or consciousness. The Ultimate- or Supreme Spirit or Energy Force will then be what most of you perceive as God or by whatever other name man chooses to refer to it. Let's stick to the names 'Ultimate Spirit' or God.

"By now you know that there was no beginning and that there will never be an end. This means that the Ultimate Spirit *has always been and will always be*. Just as matter simply exists and could never be destroyed, so the Ultimate Spirit exists, could never be destroyed and will never change. There is no need for a 'chicken and egg' discussion, as the one simply cannot exist without the other. If ever there was only nothing, then God Himself didn't exist – 'no-thing' means exactly that."

I started to counter. "Yes, but... ahh... OK, never mind..." I couldn't argue against that and realized that Teecha was slowly laying bare my deepest beliefs, my own self. He was opening up long forgotten memory files, which contained confusion and many unanswered questions. It was truly frightening but at the same time exciting, and he was obviously aware of my concerns.

"If the Ultimate Spirit could exist with nothing else around, it means that 'some-thing', God Himself, already existed and thus everything else, because 'everything else' IS God! The following is said in your Bible, Exodus 3 verse 14: "I AM THAT I AM". According to the script, that was the answer Moses received when he asked about God's name. If you think that Descartes's saying makes some sense, even when taken to mean no more than 'Thought Is', then you needn't worry anymore about the Ultimate Spirit's existence."

Once again he stunned me into deep thought but I knew he wasn't finished – there were many more unanswered questions and unsolved mysteries in my mind. Teecha himself was the latest.

"Yesterday Ace, we discussed the fact that creation is an ongoing process that could never stop. The following is written in the Qur'an, Sura X verse 4: '*It is He who beginneth the process of creation, and repeateth it...*'

"Consider the fact that the Orion nebula or star-cloud contains enough matter for something in the order of 10,000 stars. It is like a maternity home where stars will be born or created – yet it is a drop in the ocean compared to the rest of the universe. The word 'creation' should not be used for a beginning of something which never was, but for something which is eternally happening, right now, all the time, and, the Ultimate Spirit and everything else exist within and as a part of this never-ending process."

He continued his explanation: "Just as matter exists in all forms, shapes and sizes imaginable, likewise the Ultimate Spirit exists in any conceivable form and we're part of it all, hence the term '*created in the image of God*'... This is something that humans, as spirits on a reasonably high level of awareness, instinctively know. Not all of you will agree, as your perception of God and being-ness differs drastically. However, you all have instincts and you all have knowledge and skills that were not necessarily acquired through learning. Some of you have a natural inclination for understanding mathematics, while others have no difficulty playing musical instruments or creating beautiful art."

I understood this and found it a perplexing question. "Teecha, that's something I accepted in my own life but still I don't understand it. Why is it so?"

He answered obliquely. "For many years bats were seen as creatures from the devil, because man didn't understand how it was possible that they could fly and hunt for food in total darkness. Today you know that they have a 'super-sense' of echo sounding which is similar to radar. Homing pigeons have something similar insofar as using the magnetic waves of the earth to guide them back to a loft. The common goldfish can see far more of the light spectrum than most other beings. Dogs have super-senses, bloodhounds have a famous sense of smell and most dogs hear things you'll never do. Some humans have unusual knowledge or extraordinary senses, which you call 'Extra Sensory Perception' or ESP.

"This quote from the Qur'an, Sura II verse 31, may indicate how you acquired your deeper knowledge: '*And He (God) taught Adam the nature of all things; then he placed them before the Angels, and said: Tell Me the nature of these if ye are right.*'" He explained: "From the Arabic text, commentators translate that man (the name Adam means man, therefore the reference to 'them') was taught the inner nature and qualities of all things, 'things' include feelings and emotions. Man was thus able to understand and appreciate things like love, and to plan and initiate, as God made him the vice-regent of Earth. So far he made a lousy job of it!

"The crux of the matter Ace, is that man has knowledge, instincts and emotions. This is the reason why you as spirits rather than physical beings further your pursuit of knowledge and experience, why you question your existence and why you communicate. However, there's more to it. Firstly, spirits don't exist in known material forms, but as energy forces or something the like. Any spirit (or ghost for that matter) has to exist as something – it cannot be nothing. As your scientists have a good time christening particles with fancy names, how about a '*spiriton*' for the stuff spirits are made of?"

He had a secretive smile as he reached for his bag and took out the *Se!warra'warra*, which he put down next to him, carefully, as if it was a very expensive instrument. Whenever he played it, it looked as if he was smoking a pipe, producing no smoke but sound like a bagpipe, so I decided to call it his 'pipe'. I had trouble in pronouncing the click-clack word anyway.

Teecha continued: "Anyway Ace, in that particular form, such a spirit merely exists and is unable to experience physical feelings and emotions which are required for growth to higher planes of existence. A spirit has to materialize, in other words, to use or control some form of matter to express and experience its existence. As such, any spirit has a basic urge to attach itself to a form of matter for a certain period or time. This attaching of a spirit to matter is the wonder of what we call 'life' – indeed, the greatest wonder. Now, depending on the level of consciousness of any spirit and what it wants and needs to grow to or experience, its choice of a life form could be anything, anywhere: large or small, beautiful or ugly, stately or comical, perfect or deformed, happy or miserable, good or evil..." I interjected. "Life is a wonderful thing, Teecha, and from what you've told me it is obvious that you believe in spirits – in fact, I'm starting to do so myself with you around... But anyway, what makes you so sure that a spirit is an entity which attaches itself to a life form? Isn't an organism all there is to it – it thinks, sleeps, eats and drinks which means 'it is' and it lives – why do you talk about a spirit as something which is divorced from life?"

I thought my question was rather clever but he made that sound again. "*Tchi... tchi...* No spirit, no life – take those words any which way you choose. All life forms have a basic building block, the DNA molecule or Deoxyribonucleic Acid. This is, of course, just another arrangement of matter. DNA molecules contain the blueprint of what the basic or lowest form of life, a single cell, is to become. The information stored in this

DNA molecule, which by the way makes a joke of your biggest computers, determines whether that cell will stay a single cell, like the amoeba, or divide and grow into a collection of cells which then become an organism."

I interrupted: "Teecha, our latest computers are extremely powerful, capable of executing millions of instructions per second – in my mind that's no joke but a fantastic technological achievement!"

He replied patiently: "Ace, should you instruct all of earth's most powerful computers to formulate only one type of DNA molecule capable of creating life, by finding the right combination given all the possibilities of four complex molecules called nucleotides, each consisting of more than 30 atoms linked in a particular way, you're going to wait an awful long time. The odds of any computer coming up with just one such a DNA molecule could be likened to a 6 coming up every time in 140 throws of a dice. The probability against this is in the order of 10 to the power of approximately 110. If those were gambling odds, the devil would have no business.

"Given all the time since Earth's creation and allowing for the fact that your computers **do** execute millions of instructions per second, none of them would have had enough time to find the right structure for one DNA molecule."

Mathematically he was right once more: Life didn't happen by chance. "Hang on," I said and scratched in the sand. "Incredible stuff Teecha. Every living organism is a miracle – more so when I think that each of us have our own character. But your attaching spirit story is ..."

"Something you find difficult to believe?" he finished my sentence for me.

I smiled. "Eheh."

He grinned. "Ace, an organism could be very primitive, for lack of better words, such as lichen, or highly intelligent such as man. Each and every organism has its own special arrangement of DNA within its cells. However, no matter how sophisticated such an organism is and how wonderful the process of growing from a single cell may be, the organism itself consists of nothing but matter: Without an *'I'* or spirit, it is as dead as a doornail."

He was more than serious. "Only when a spirit attaches itself to such an organism does the organism live, can it move around, use its senses, reproduce more organisms, and most importantly, experience and pursue its own needs. A spirit uses an organism as a vehicle to achieve its objectives, and once those have been achieved, the organism itself, in whatever form it existed, is of no more use to the spirit. It will simply detach itself from that organism which will then 'die' or disintegrate. But there's a bit more to it:

"Time, in the context of eternity, doesn't exist – there is no such thing. How can there be time if there is no beginning and no end? Only because of the existence of matter and space and the fact that all matter is in constant motion, time becomes relative. It can then be measured on some scale to determine nothing else than the interval between one event and the next. You call the interval between regular events of the sun rising 24 hours or one day, the interval between one summer and the next a year, and what is required for light to travel 12 inches a nanosecond. Man is known to live for 'three score years and ten', while some plants like the *welwitchia mirabilis* found in the Namib desert, or the giant redwood trees of California, live for up to 2,500 years.

"Now you want to know what's the meaning of all this, right?"

I gave a nod and so did Teecha, confirming what he knew anyway.

"Let me repeat that a spirit attaches itself to an organism. This is the start of an event for that particular spirit, for which only a specific interval of time is required in which to experience what it needs at its level of consciousness at that instant. At human level, most of you still lack the ability to spiritually control matter. Higher life forms are capable of doing so, for instance by disintegrating at some place and reappearing at another, and in any particular form they want to. There are many recorded cases of such appearances. One example is the Bible, in Acts 1 verse 10:

'They were looking intently up into the sky as He was going, when suddenly two men dressed in white stood beside them...'

"However, at lower levels of consciousness a spirit will do everything possible to remain attached to its organism for the full duration of that life-event. This is to ensure that it will achieve the experiences and spiritual growth required in that life. The urge to remain attached to an organism is none other than what you call the survival instinct. If an organism is damaged beyond repair the spirit has to leave it and the organism dies. To prevent this from happening prematurely, spirits with similar material bodies and levels of consciousness team up to ensure survival of the species. That way they enhance each individual spirit's chances of physically surviving any particular event, thus gaining more experience and knowledge during that lifetime."

Teecha went to fetch a mug of water and I used the opportunity to water a dry plant. It was cold and I took a blanket to the fire. He had already added more firewood and filled the kettle, a hint for coffee, I assumed. What he had told me so far was of more immediate interest and I was eager to hear more. He didn't disappoint me.

"Another basic urge of any spirit is to create life, or actually just more organisms of its own kind," he continued once he had settled back down by the fire. "The reasons being firstly, to ensure that there will be enough organisms around for spirits of its own level to attach themselves to, and to ensure that there will be an organism available for its own future experiences. But more important is the fact that by itself, alone, like one particle of matter, it cannot exist. That's why it has an urge to create life, to ensure for itself the experience of life to the fullest. This basic instinct to create life manifests itself in the sexual drive to reproduce, which is nothing else but to ensure spiritual survival. Sex has become more than that – it could be the primitive instinct, an act of true love, plain lust or something in-between, depending on the situation.

"However, there is more to life **after** life, life **before** life and life **between** life than you've cared to think about." He knew how to entice my curiosity but I decided not to ask what he meant. In time he was going to tell me anyway because I had realized that he realized that I knew that he knew exactly what I wanted to know... Something to that effect. Fully aware by then that he sensed my thoughts, it didn't concern me in the least.

"The higher the level of existence of a spirit, the more complex its life-events become. Experiencing all sorts of emotions becomes important. It eventually acquires the capability to distinguish between good and evil, which throws a spanner into the works. But apart from anything else, the spirit is now obsessed with emotions and will try them all: love, fear, anger, hate, happiness, misery, boredom, excitement, you name it. In fact, it will seek out and bring upon itself emotions not yet experienced."

"Are you telling me that a spirit has more than one life, and that it experiences or learns something in each before getting another go at it? What for? Is it like – " He held up his hand.

"Eheh, but one thing at a time. Reincarnation has always been a subject of controversy. It would seem, though, that it is a natural part of life, which ancient peoples knew about and modern man finds more and more evidence of. The mere fact that around 70% of all people believe in life after death, suggests it is widely desired," he stated.

"More factual proof is the now rather common practice of freeing patients from neurotic disorders through a process called hypnotic regression. This technique became popular because it works. At first, psychiatrists and hypnotists alike were able to take subjects back into the past to where some traumatic experience during childhood may have caused a particular phobia or mental problem. Knowledge of that incident and its cause had the remarkable effect of ridding the incumbent of his fear or disorder, mentally and often physically. This is also known as psychoanalysis, founded by Sigmund Freud. It was however soon discovered that under hypnosis, subjects could be taken back to **many** previous lives. This fact caused various psychiatrists, after thousands of case studies, to agree that:

"Once guided to another lifetime, the hypnotic subject assumes a different personality and acknowledges a different body while being aware of sharing with this other self the same basic identity. Change of sex and race is commonplace. The past-life personality can be directed to any point between its birth and death and will often discuss freely the experiences of that lifetime in a voice that reflects its age, gender, culture, language, character and placement in historical time. When the store of emotionally significant memories from that life is exhausted, the person in trance then summons up another offshoot of the core identity – another unique personality grappling with a completely different existence."

I had to get something off my chest: "Teecha, where the hell do you come from and how do you know all this? You're not from here, are you? No, don't bother, forget that. Why are you here?"

He remained as unperturbed as before: "I've already told you where I come from and that I'll be whoever you want me to be. And just for the record, especially to racists, male chauvinists and feminists, note that *'change of sex and race is commonplace'*."

I felt like sticking out my tongue but managed to imitate his '*Tchi...tchi...*' thinking: "And so, I hear, is change of species, old man." He stared at the fire for a long time. When he resumed talking, I wasn't too sure about his sense of humor:

"It isn't funny Ace, unless you expect yourself to return as a sabre-tooth barking turkey the next time around. You have many scriptures telling you what reincarnation means, like the *Bardo Thodol*, better known as the *Tibetan Book of the Dead*, dated 800 years before Christ. There is the *Brihadaranayaka Upanishad* from India and the *Egyptian Book of the Dead*– its original title being *Bring Forth in Light* – which dates 1300 years before Christ. And there is the '*Katha Upanishad*' of India, from 700 years later. To quote from the latter:

'The Self does not die when the body dies. Concealed in the heart of all beings lies the 'atma', the Spirit, the Self; smaller than the smallest

atom, greater than the greatest spaces.'

"By the way Ace," he added suddenly, "did man discover the atom in this age?" His question must have been rhetorical so I didn't answer.

"Rebirth is the underlying doctrine of most religions," he continued, "whether taught that there is only one spiritual life hereafter or many more to come. If you believe in reincarnation or resurrection, in other words in another life after death, there may just as well be many such lives, especially if you consider that eternity has time to spare.

"Scientific and psychoanalytic investigations, apart from the scriptures, suggest that a spirit has more than one life. The state of existence between death and a spirit's next physical life, is described in *The Tibetan Book of the Dead* as the '*Bardo'*."

The kettle was singing away and I got up to make coffee. Teecha picked up his pipe, stretched his legs and walked a few meters to the perimeter of the firelight where he started playing it. Facing the darkness his body slowly danced to the rhythm of a song unknown to me, which sent weird tunes into the night. That strange, disturbing feeling of déjà vu, realizing that you are at a place you know very well but physically couldn't have been there before, was very strong. I was positive I had seen Teecha standing just like that, playing his pipe, sometime before... No, it must have been then and there – the scene was too familiar. I kept on listening. When he paused again, I shoved my emotions aside and called him for coffee. I realized with surprise that I had made it without being aware of doing so; tasting it for sugar, I handed him a mug.

"Teecha, you seem to be sure of a spiritual life and it certainly sounds feasible from all those facts. But even if it is so, for what reasons then – why can't we just live one life and get done with it?"

There was a long noisy sip and then he clicked his tongue. "I mentioned that a spirit at human level wants and needs to experience all possible emotions and to gain spiritual growth. It is unlikely to achieve all of that in a lifetime of 70 to 80 years, should you be lucky to survive that long. This in itself suggests that you'll need more time – probably a few lifetimes. When a spirit reaches the human level of existence, together with his newfound knowledge of good and evil, it conducts experiments and plays games and wins some and loses some. As part of its spiritual adventures it has multiple choices. As it becomes proficient at the game it sees a few moves ahead, like a good chess player does. But in this case the opponent is Life, always with a few surprises up her sleeve..."

"There are rules and tactics to all games and to become a 'pro' requires some coaching. For advice on how to live, it associates with spirits at its own or higher levels through many life events, to acquire the necessary experience and knowledge. It needs other spirits to teach it – or rather to show it – what in fact it already knows: All of you know more than you think you do, you merely need to accept and to understand what you already know."

"At humans' level, association with other spirits shows itself in many ways, like society and norms, culture, religion, family and sport. It also shows in the choice of a mate, friends and work environment. You say people are spiritually attracted, there is a bond between them or that they are 'soul mates'. All this means is that most spirits need other spirits to help them along. Somehow you always find them.

"What's more, at human levels of consciousness, some spirits realize their spiritual existence and try to gain experiences not related to their present physical forms. As it says in 1 Thessalonians 5 verse 21, you are free to *'Test everything and to hold on to the good'*, aren't you Ace?"

"Yes, I suppose so. Now correct me if I'm wrong: to experience and understand everything there is will probably take a little longer than eternity, unless like you say, we have some guidance. And provided we live more than once, to experience death and other states of consciousness too. It all seems a bit complicated to me – will we ever get there?"

Teecha looked pleased for a change. "Apart from the spirit's awareness of its own self, there are other types of consciousness. One of these is termed collective consciousness – every living thing is conscious of other spirits around it, whether they exist in a material form or not, whether they be good or evil or whether they are primitive or highly intelligent. We are aware of one another, and dependant on each other. The mere fact that you are aware of material spirits around you right now – like the nightjar who just called, or that chirping cricket – is proof of this.

"The fact that you may not be able to perceive immaterial spiritual beings with your normal senses, or that you have not yet proved the existence of extraterrestrials, is no reason to deny their being. Most of you know about them subconsciously, which on occasion turns your skin into gooseflesh or makes the hair in the back of your neck stand on end.

"Another type is super-consciousness or universal consciousness. Many philosophers have discussed the subject and most religions suggest such a state of complete awareness in the afterlife.

"As it says in the Bible, 1 Corinthians 13 verse 12:

'*For now we see through a glass, darkly; but then face to face: now I know in part; but then shall I know even as also I am known.*'

"During investigations on regression to past lives, it was found that incumbents often experienced a state of awareness they could hardly describe in words afterwards. This was so extraordinary that it was termed '*Metaconsciousness*':

'A supremely paradoxical state of memory awareness in which the percipient loses all sense of personal identity by merging into existence itself, only to become more intensely self-aware than ever.

To experience metaconsciousness is to reach beyond three-dimensional reality to learn one's reason for being ...'

"This awareness is the reason why man dreams about becoming, and strives to become, like the Ultimate Spirit. Your religions furnish you with the Dos and Don'ts of how to achieve it and some of you perceive that final stage to be heaven. If heaven with its pearly gates or hell with the devil's fork were all there is to life, what could be more boring? Ace, deep inside you know as well as I do that there is much, much more – if only you would tune in to the all encompassing life force, if you unchain yourself from useless and rotten beliefs, if you overcome your fears and explore new ideas and horizons. If you'd only realize that:

We are all there for each other, dependant on one another and all a part of one great organism, ONE Spirit."

******

'... All (man and the animals) have the same breath (or spirit);
man has no advantage over the animal... All go to the same place; all come from dust, and to dust all return.
Who knows if the spirit of man rises upward and if the spirit of the animal goes down into the earth?'

Ecclesiastes 3:19-21

******

THE FOURTH DAY

"See you in the morning, my friend."

It was the first time Teecha had called me his friend and it instilled a certain calmness in my rather confused spirit. It was long past midnight and I yawned loudly.

"Goodnight… and thank you, Teecha."

Closing the tent flap I realized for the first time that I hadn't seen Xi'tau all evening. To be sure, I opened the flap again and looked around. Teecha lay underneath the umbrella thorn all by himself with his head on his elbow, already fast asleep. Xi'tau was nowhere to be seen. Crawling back into the tent, I experienced a strange yet familiar fatherly emotion, actual concern with a lion's whereabouts.

I lay on my back for a long time, staring at the darkness inside the tent. Slowly but surely a menacing whirlpool formed which drew me closer and closer. In growing panic I tried to swim away but even my last frantic efforts were useless. It sucked me in and spiraled me down a dark tunnel.

Images of frightened and fleeing springbok rushed past. A giant lion stormed snarling towards me – the blow from his sharp-nailed forepaw sent me spinning through space.

Then I was a young boy of six, opening a farm gate. A black mamba raised itself up in front of me, its slitty eyes ten inches (20 centimeters) from mine, with a forked tongue lisping in and out, in and out.

"Keep still. Don't move!" somebody shouted. I wanted to move but I couldn't if I tried.

Far off a shot sounded. This was a strange snake, blood dripping from its ears, which formed a small puddle right by my feet. I didn't know snakes bleed through their ears. Mesmerized, I watched as the mamba's eyes slowly turned dull, then its body twisted around and around. In the next second my father grabbed me away from the snake. His .22 rifle killing it from meters away and saving my life. Then he was gone, leaving me alone again.

A hunter with a powerful and telescopically sighted rifle appeared from the void. I sighed with relief, at least there was somebody to help me, and shouted: "Here! Over here..."

He heard me and rushed over – thank goodness. Then a petrifying shock – his eyes belonged to Death. I panicked and rushed for cover but too late – he aimed and fired. An excruciating pain ripped through my spine. With a loud scream I crashed to the ground.

Suddenly there were darkly crawling, groaning shapes: hissing snakes, birds with razor sharp beaks and animals with groping claws and snapping jaws, all trying to get at me crying: "Why... What for?"

I knew the answer: The spirits of all the animals I had hunted, stealing their gift of life, were after my own. Terrified, I tried to flee but couldn't move, my back was shattered by the bullet. With blood all over me, I fought them off with hands and teeth but I was totally outnumbered. Feeling tired and weak, I was suddenly outside my own body, but still attached to it. Looking down, I was helplessly paralyzed, while the creatures clawed and ripped me to pieces.

"No. No. Stop it! You can't do that," I shouted defiantly, but to no avail. A dim light appeared from the midst of my darkest self, growing brighter and brighter.

Then a loud shout:

"Who's that? Dad? Dad, help me, please..."

The mamba opened its black mouth, baring long poisonous fangs, ready to strike that fatal bite. Somebody gripped me by the shoulders and jerked me away from the bleeding snake, exactly as it happened at the gate and into the light.

Still struggling with the demons of my mind, I slowly opened my eyes.

"Ace! Are you OK?" The Bushman knelt over me, looking very concerned in the torchlight. I shivered in a cold sweat.

"No... Ahhh ... Yes. It's OK, I'm fine, thanks," I managed.

Without another word, Teecha bluntly left me and I continued to battle with my own emotions, feeling very sorry for myself and thinking that there's never anybody around to talk to when you really need it. However, a few minutes later Teecha returned and handed me a mug of liquid that closely resembled fermented pea soup, and commanded: "Here, drink up – it'll sort your mind out..."

It must have done just that, for it tasted like my dream and then knocked me out stone cold.

Before sunrise I was up again but there was little peace in my mind. Trying to regain some reality, I washed the dishes, rearranged everything and swept all the dry leaves from the camp area. Like the past few mornings, Teecha was not around, although he had already made the fire. I checked the vehicle's oil and water. All OK. I untied two jerry cans of fuel and spent ten minutes looking for the funnel. Finally, finding it exactly where I always keep it, I had to stop and ask myself what was happening.

Lost in thought, I poured my third cup of coffee then slid down the side of the vehicle, my heels digging two little furrows in the sand as I tried to balance the mug and to wiggle a seat into the cold sand simultaneously. I leaned back onto the vehicle's tire and burnt my lips with the steaming mug.

"Dammit, what the hell am I doing? I must be going out of my mind." Putting the mug aside, I got up again and started to empty the contents of the first jerry can, battling to keep the funnel in place at the same time.

"Are you leaving?"

By now I was used to his unexpected appearances, but I was upset and without thinking, I snapped: "Where the hell have you been?"

"*Ke gona*," he replied calmly, "and I was here last night too."

"Yes, I know that... Uhmm... Thanks, Teecha. I'm sorry, I didn't mean that. I have many things on my mind."

"Eheh – it's troubled too. Let's walk."

He set off into the bush again, this time in a totally different direction. "Troubled my foot," I mumbled, but before he had disappeared I called: "Wait, I'll be with you now."

That day he showed and taught me many things. The medicinal and other uses of plant leaves and roots, and the behavior and habits of various animals and birds. He showed me where to find the Kalahari sun beetles and how they made that ear-piercing noise. He showed me where the Bushmen find the deadly poison for their arrows. Apart from using snake venom, milk-sap from toxic plants like the *euphorbia*, crushed scorpion tails and button spiders, the most virulent poison they use is obtained from the larvae of *diamphilia-* and *polyclada* beetles. These beetles feed on the leaves of the *marula* and *commiphora* trees, the latter locally known as a '*kanniedood*', which translated means: 'cannot die'. The name is obviously derived from the tree's ability to withstand severe drought and extreme temperatures. The beetle cocoons are found in the sand underneath the trees, and their bodily juices are extremely toxic.

As was the case with many other types of plants, the *kanniedood* had various other uses. For instance, the gum and resins from the tree are used for abdominal pains and fever. They are mixed with animal fat to make a body lotion and insect repellant, especially effective against termites. The bark is used as an antidote against snakebite and the fruit for stomach ailments. The soft but strong stems are used to construct traps for various animals, including leopard and lion.

"Just another tree," I had thought before.

Around lunchtime we rested in the shade of a shepherd's tree. Hardly anything to write home about, to me it was once more just another tree. However, its bark was conspicuously white and it had dark green leathery leaves.

"This is called the 'Tree of Life'," Teecha remarked.

"How come?"

"First of all, the older trees' trunks are hollow inside, and catch rainwater for many animals and birds. The evergreen leaves are very nourishing for game and livestock. The roots can be dried, roasted and ground for coffee, which tastes just like yours, or it can be pounded into a meal to make porridge. The wood is heavy and strong, and is used to make various utensils – like my digging stick. Sap from the crushed leaves is used as an ointment for inflamed eyes. If you break a stem or even chop the tree off, it will simply grow again."

When Teecha paused, I wondered for how long there would be people around who knew about the natural uses and remedies of plants, insects and other things like he did. That knowledge is verbally passed on from one generation to the next and with the Bushmen nearly extinct, mankind is losing it. However, I sensed that he had more to say about the tree.

"It is said that if you dig around its roots at sunrise, and find a root which points directly to the rising sun, you can pound that root to make a brew. When you drink it that night, you will meet your would-be wife or husband in a dream. If however, you dig around the other side of the tree, and find a root that points directly to the setting sun, you can brew that root for a dream that will point out all your enemies..."

"Fascinating, but superstitious nonsense," I thought.

"It is also said that if you burn the wood, your cows will only produce bull calves."

"Come on Teecha, do you believe all that?"

"There are many things in the minds of people, Ace, some extremely positive and powerful, some negative and detrimental. Over the last few days your own has been troubled about things you cannot explain or do not know about.

"I'd like to tell you a few things about the mind for it is one of the greatest powers in the universe. You see, the mind is the spirit and the spirit is the mind, but every spirit has many different minds, so are there minds consisting of many spirits..."

******

THE MIND

"Like a circle in a spiral,
like a wheel within a wheel,
never ending or beginning,
on an ever spinning reel...
like the circles that you find,
in the windmills of your mind."

from the song *'The Windmills of Your Mind'*

"Hang on, Teecha. You're saying the spirit and the mind is one and the same but that each consists of many of the other? That's pushing logic – what shall I try instead?"

With his hand on his brow, he stared at the plain in front of us. In the distance was what I assumed to be a herd of wildebeest. From where we sat I could only see a mass of animals obscured in dust.

Not getting any response from Teecha, I wasn't too sure whether he had heard me, even when he stood up after a while and said: "Let's go, Ace – we'll talk on the way."

He picked up his spears and set off towards the plain. When we reached the edges of it I fell in next to him. The grass on the plain was dry-green and grazed short for that time of the year. There were only scattered patches of trees and no thorn shrubs. It was like walking on an enormous golf course where one could only get into the rough with great difficulty. What a dream.

"Come on Teecha, you said you'd tell me about the mind – now what did you mean with those many minds?"

He kept on walking in the direction of the wildebeest as if to get ahead of them. Finally he replied:

"Mind is an insignificant little word, yet it has many different meanings. You say: 'Mind your own business', 'Mind your step!' 'Bear in mind that...' 'It slipped my mind' or 'Do you mind?' and you often ask: 'Are you out of your mind?' What do you mean when you use it?"

When he answered his own question with another, I sensed his mood and listened.

"Could it be that you know the meaning; what it really implies? Eheh, you all do, because you use it to express exactly what you mean and you all know just when to use it. What do you mean?

My mouth opened but I shut it in time, sticking to my decision to listen. He continued:

"Maybe something like this: Memory or remembrance, intellect, reason, intelligence, will power, moral, ethical, intellectual outlook, cognitive power, volitional capacities, view, opinion, thought, intension, desire, pay attention to, care about, heed, object, be careful. 'Mind' means many different things. You also have another word for similar concepts. It describes the non-material, divine element that gives humans life and reason, the soul, will and intelligence divorced from the body, an immaterial being possessing cognition, a ghost, an influence, personal qualities, courage, pride or the fundamental principle or true meaning of something."

I ignored my decision to listen. "Teecha, if I'm not mistaken, the word 'spirit' also means a potent mind-confusing liquor, true?"

"Eheh, Ace, no wonder you attach the same word to it – and seeing that you know what a liquid spirit is all about, consider then the power of a real one."

Gone was my attempted wit. "OK, Teecha, forget it. What then is the difference between the 'mind' and the 'spirit'?"

"Not much – both words refer to the same thing which consists of many different entities."

Once more he had made me think, but he tested my patience too. "So…? True – now that *really* makes sense..."

He ignored my sarcasm. "Ace, if you freely substitute the words 'mind' and 'spirit' in a sentence, then with a little imagination you will come to the same understanding. How's this for a try: 'To have presence of spirit', 'To be in two spirits', 'Get into the mind of the party', 'Spirit your step!' or 'Put some mind into it!' Does that make sense?"

The words didn't sound so good when used in that way but he had made his point. I replied: "Yes, but it's poor English."

He remained unconcerned and then either shocked me back into or completely out of reality – I felt somewhere in-between after his next words:

"I wouldn't know that – I don't speak it."

The click-clack of Khoisan ricocheted in my ears and I stopped dead. All of a sudden I was alone in the middle of a vast expanse, with nothing around but grass, and a few meters ahead, in a haze, an old Bushman moving like the wind. Unreal. A cold fear gripped me – he was indeed unreal and I was completely alone not knowing where to go. I didn't even know in which direction the camp was. As if he was a mirage that would soon disappear, I raced after him.

When I caught up only a few meters further ahead, he continued as if I had stayed behind just to tie a bootlace:

"Ace, the mind is one of the most discussed and most misunderstood subjects of all times, for the simple reason that you fail to see the connection between your 'mind' and your 'spirit'. For thousands of years man has recognized the fact that he has a brain. He knows that when his brain is seriously damaged his body dies. Likewise if his body is damaged beyond repair his brain quickly follows suit, after which the whole organism is 'clinically dead'. Yet his body can survive major disasters. It could lose all its limbs, it could lose sight and hearing, it could lose or even have organs replaced and still function. Damage to his brain however, is more serious.

"Although certain parts of it may be surgically reduced without repercussions, removing vital parts or incurring irreparable damage to some regions of the brain has a certain and predictable effect on the organism. It took modern man a long time to rediscover ancient knowledge, but to date he has identified almost all regions of the brain which control the specific functions of an organism; whether that may be for his own type of body or for many other life forms. Incidentally, Ace, humans acquired much of this knowledge at the expense of other lives, like mice, guinea pigs and baboons, and at the expense of lives of his own kind. He is still expending life for that purpose, and worse, for his own comfort and to please his taste buds, making man the cruelest and most vicious animal on earth."

Something subconscious compelled me to defend mankind, although my deepest self told me I had no leg to stand on. Even as I spoke I knew the words were not from my heart:

"That's not true. Without research we would never have been able to prevent disease or to provide cures for both man and animal, and you also eat meat – very few of us are vegetarians."

"Ace, there are better ways to do research and so far man's ways have succeeded only in destroying his own future. However, before you get emotional, consider the following: even if all of you were dedicated vegetarians, you would still kill to eat. When you pick a flower, cook a cabbage or bite a juicy apple, you kill life or potential life. On the other hand, your eating that apple may actually assist the creation of more life. Some plants evolved in such a clever and unique way, that their seeds have to be eaten by some animal, digested and excreted before they will germinate and grow. A good example of this is the nuts of the *makalani* palm, which is almost exclusively 'planted' by elephants. Apart from that, you all kill – by spraying insecticide into the air or swatting a fly. Every time you breathe, your body wipes out hundreds of living but potentially dangerous microscopic organisms."

"But that's not the same, Teecha," I interrupted, "and we don't kill animals for the fun of it – we have to eat too."

"What's the difference between killing an ox or catching a trout, Ace? A life is a life. Xi'tau is a fortunate example of man's fun and games. Your eating of animals is not the problem though – it's the way you do it: Some of you use a specially 'blessed' golden knife to slit the jugular veins of so called 'clean' animals, after which they are left to bleed to death. You breed and transport animals under atrocious conditions and in confinements worse than any of your jails. You'll need a lot of guts to go into any of your modern slaughter houses and you'll need to wear gumboots to stop you from slipping as you wade through inches of blood."

There is no defense against the truth. We walked a few meters in silence and Teecha kept up a brisk pace, straight towards the wildebeest.

I prodded: "You were telling me about the brain?"

As usual, he continued as if there had been no change of subject.

"Without going too deeply into its biological facts and features, consider the basics: All living organisms have a brain except for plants – so you think. The higher a spirit's level of consciousness, the more complex and important the brain of its 'vehicle' is. In advanced life forms you can distinguish various parts of the brain, like the brain stem, consisting of the medulla oblongata, pons, midbrain and thalamus, the cerebrum, the cerebellum and the ventricles, and the cerebral cortex. The latter is a very prominent part and the center for higher correlations and intellectual activity like that in humans. The whole of the brain is connected by a multitude of nerve fibers that connect 'sensory' and 'motor' nerves throughout the body. There is a mass of nerve fibers called the corpus callosum, connecting the two completely divided cerebral hemispheres. These two halves of the brain are called the left brain and right brain respectively.

"Exactly which parts of the brain handle your normal senses like sight, smell, taste, hearing and touch have been identified – even down to which part controls an eye, arm, leg, hand or the tongue. It is known which parts control and facilitate such complex aspects as understanding speech and reading.

"The more complex mental processes are located in the frontal region of the cerebral cortex and neurology suggests that the left brain handles more of the analytical, mathematical and logical thought processes, while the right brain handles intuition, abstract and lateral thoughts, as well as art, music and creativity."

He paused before continuing:

"What really takes place in the brain, Ace, is difficult to understand. Man is very busy creating artificial intelligence, building and testing AI computers. For any such computer, it will probably be extremely difficult to compute how it itself operates, let alone to understand who built it and why. It has been found though, that the brain reacts to exercise much in the same way as the body: Muscles become strong and fit with regular exercise and develop in size. The same principle goes for the brain with mental exercise. It doesn't become physically bigger, like muscles do, but it increases the number of 'neuron connections' it has. This was discovered through laboratory experiments with rats. The brains of rats who had been stimulated to experience many different things in their environment showed many more neuron connections than those of their peers who were forced to lead a dull life. Microscopic analysis of Einstein's brain showed that his brain had many more neuron connections than that of the average human."

By then I knew Teecha well enough to realize that he was mentioning those biological facts for a reason. At the time, though, he was walking purposefully towards the wildebeest, still about 400 meters away. Every now and then he stopped and gazed intently at them through squinting eyes. The animals were not grazing as I had thought, but moving at a fair pace in a northeasterly direction. I had heard about their migrating habits but never realized that they do it in such large numbers.

Teecha seemed preoccupied with the animals but I was eager to hear more about the mind, so I asked:

"Why are you walking towards them? There must be close on 3,000 wildebeest and we're on foot. If we frighten them they may stampede and then I wouldn't like to be around..."

"They won't do anything to you, Ace, except to show you how the mind works. Come!"

"How the h..." but I swallowed my words.

Teecha carried on talking and left me baffled as to how wildebeest could have any relevance.

"In relation to his body size, man's frontal cortex is much larger than that of most other living organisms. Strangely, it seems that the function of the frontal cortex is inter alia to inhibit or prevent free expression of the higher senses. 'Higher senses' in this context purporting such things as judgment, morals, sex, love, hate and even anger or fear. Animals express these senses and emotions freely, while humans are apparently better equipped to control or inhibit them.

"This astonishing fact was discovered by way of the surgical process lobotomy, the term used for incising or detaching parts of the brain in an effort to reduce abnormalities. It was found that individuals on whom a frontal lobotomy had been performed, developed an easygoing and uninhibited mode of existence, while on the other hand they lost higher standards and judgment, intellectually and morally. Lobotomics are cruelly continuing in the name of research but this has led to a significant discovery.

"Firstly, it was found that patients with severe brain damage, like that caused by serious accidents, may recover sufficiently to lead a reasonably normal life. Yet, their orientation to the present and their memory of very recent events is almost nonexistent. Recall of the past before the accident, however, is usually excellent. Secondly, the same discovery was made through intentional surgery on patients suffering from severe epilepsy. It was found that when the corpus callosum (that part of the brain connecting the two half-brains) was severed, they suffered no further epileptic attacks. They could lead normal lives with no loss of intellect, personality or IQ. They also had excellent memories – but only of the past, before their operations. Once again their orientation to the present and their memory of anything that happened five minutes ago became nonexistent.

"The discovery of this fact, Ace, naturally led to more research. You found that an organism's brain could be cut away to leave but the bare essentials to maintain the bodily functions, yet memory of the past was always there. In most cases though, no new impressions of the present could be remembered at all... Obviously, excessive brain damage or degeneration of brain cells which impair important centers of the brain will lead to so-called memory loss, as the brain unit as a whole will then be malfunctioning. Anyway, after this some frantic research was done to find the location of memory in an organism's brain, human or not human. To date, there's been no success."

The wildebeest had seen us. Teecha was walking towards the front of the herd, as if he intended to head them off. They were moving in a V-shape, the rear end of the herd was directly to our left but at least half a kilometer away. The lead animal was slightly ahead of us and to the right. It was still too far to see clearly but I assumed he was a bull. He stopped and stared at us and Teecha stared back at him. A few other animals also stopped and looked rather agitated – they milled around, snorted and kicked up dust with their hooves, most certainly sharing my own unhappiness.

Teecha merely said: "Ace, don't look at them directly. Follow me." He set off again at a faster pace, this time moving towards the right. As he did so the leader continued walking and the others followed him without further anxiety. That didn't soothe my own nerves because if Teecha carried on in the direction he had taken, we would meet up with the leader very soon – in fact, we would end up right in front of him.

"Teecha, I hope you know what you're doing... but still I don't think it is wise. These animals must be migrating somewhere and that's all they have on their mind. It'll be dangerous to get in their way."

He ignored me so I kept on glancing at them.

"Ace, with the latest experiments it was found that whenever you access your memory the center of your brain becomes active. There is nothing special about the center of a brain – in fact, you have no name for it, as there is no specific unit or organ in the middle of the brain. It was found, though, that it 'lights up', just like your cartoons show a flashing electric bulb whenever one of the characters has a brain wave. It is postulated that the brain as a whole has access to all memory, or any part of it does, like a hologram. So, where is your memory stored? Unless your absent 'spirited' professors change their minds, they will not find it."

He winked at me and I replied with a muffled laugh: "You seem to know that, Teecha – so where is it?"

"To explain what memory is, let's take a modern computer as an example. It consists of many different units, like input/output processors, local or remote disc drives, optical scanners, bar-code sensors, printers, video display screens and, of course, a memory.

"The computer's hard drive memory is a very small unit, usually consisting of silicon chips. This unit, no bigger than the size of a credit card in modern computers, stores millions of characters of data. You talk about the memory size of computers in megabytes, where one megabyte or Mb is equal to one million 'bytes' or characters.

"A character is something like each letter in a book. If an average book contains 50,000 words and if each word has an average of 6 letters, then it would take up 300,000 bytes, not even one third of a megabyte. The internal memory of a medium range computer has between 512 and 1024 megabytes. Apart from this, its external memory size, such as the disc drives, is denoted in gigabytes or Gb, where one Gb is equal to 1,000,000,000 – one thousand million characters. Personal computers that can store 80 to 320 Gb of data are commonplace. This means that what you call a 'mini' computer could easily store all the information in a library consisting of 100,000 books or more, and it is capable of processing millions of instructions every second.

"When you compare human brains to computers there are some astonishing similarities, probably because you created computers in your own image. A brain also consists of separate units like a computer. It has 'processors' which allow for input and output of data, just like a computer: Your eyes may be likened to an input device such as an optical character reader. When you talk or write something down, it could be compared to the printed output of a computer. When you make decisions based on data available to you, from your memory or otherwise, it is similar to a computer making decisions based on the data in its memory."

We were little more than 150 meters away from the spear-point of the herd of migrating wildebeest. Teecha slowed down his pace but moved steadily closer to the leader, who kept his pace. By then I could see that it was a rather big bull and that he was limping slightly. I found it difficult to believe, but the herd was now definitely ignoring us, although we were in full sight across the grassy plain. A huge cloud of dust drifted away from them and the ground vibrated softly from thousands of hooves, a continuous droning sound like distant thunder. I was in no mood to say anything – the sight was awe-inspiring. As if in a dream I listened to Teecha, still talking away:

"The various units that your computers are made of are referred to as 'hardware'. This hardware cannot do a thing by itself without something called 'software'. Software is the programs written by humans and is often built into the hardware, which gets the tin-brain to work. 'Operating' software is the programs which make the machine appear to be alive and tells it what it consists of and under what principles it operates. The heart of this is called the 'bios' or life-chip. On the other hand, 'application' software is the programs written by humans to tell the computer how and from which units it must accept data, how to calculate and process it and what to do with the answers obtained. Application software also tells the computer when and how to update its memory banks with any calculated information, which can then be retrieved whenever necessary.

"Like a computer's hardware, the human body is dead and of no use unless it has operating software in the form of a spirit – its own 'bios chip', which makes it alive. The brain is the central processor, while intelligence, reason, judgment and choice will be the application software of the human mind, telling you how to process the data in your memory, what decisions and actions to take and what information should be updated in your memory banks..."

I took my gaze off the lead animal and brought my attention back to him.

"Teecha, that's interesting stuff but I don't see what computers have to do with us right now, except that my own software thinks we should get the hell out of here and my body is ready to obey! I have no quarrel with these wildebeest – why are you walking straight into their way?"

I might as well have talked to the family of ground squirrels who had first scattered into their burrows and then reappeared one by one to watch the procession with curiosity.

"As you know Ace, one of Murphy's laws states: 'If anything can go wrong, it will'..."

"Quite true... thanks for putting my mind at ease."

He flatly ignored me. "So it is with most computers – invariably something starts to malfunction or even blow up. In most instances, though, it is a case of one or other unit that either accesses or processes the data in the computer's memory that becomes faulty. The stored information in the internal memory is usually intact or it is stored elsewhere or 'off-line'. Once the fault is discovered and the unit is repaired or replaced, data from memory can be recovered and accessed once more, after which it would be business as usual, with no 'memory loss' to the computer or loss of data.

"Like the internal and external memory of a computer, evidence from regression to the past lives of humans suggests that you too have a 'bodily' memory and a 'spiritual' memory. Spiritual memory is stored elsewhere but directly linked to your material existence and can be accessed whenever needed. Brain damage may prevent you from accessing data from your memory banks or processing it properly, seeming to indicate loss of memory, although it is still intact, somewhere. Maybe your neuro-physicists should start looking for that '*spiriton*' particle – it would be quite something to discover. Anyway Ace, memory is a part of the mind, which means it is part of the spirit.

"This is rather logical. If a spirit wants to experience things, it needs to store the memories of each lifetime somewhere and knowing very well that any organism returns to dust, memory has to remain with the spirit. If you believe in any kind of resurrection, then you will live again, and you can't be you without your own memories.

"Now, bear in mind that a spirit needs a vehicle to experience its memories. As its requirements, goals or needs increase, so it needs a faster and more powerful vehicle with a bigger 'on-board' computer (brain) with greater capacity and lots of accessories. But, just as not just anybody can jump into the cockpit of a fighter plane and fly, or take the wheel of a 30-ton truck and drive, no spirit can turn the ignition key of its sleek new machine without some training.

"The more advanced its choice of vehicle, the longer it will take to learn which buttons to push and when, so our advanced spirit goes through childhood, adolescence and its whole adult life to learn how to fly its vehicle.

"Take a good look at life and nature, Ace, and you'll see that it's true. The human baby takes longer than any other animal to become independent, although its brain develops the fastest. Fortunately, but to a great extent also unfortunately, our spirit has many tutors before it becomes a so-called adult, at which point parents, school teachers and other mentors are no longer required – or so it usually thinks. It can now press most buttons itself. Depending on the qualifications of its instructors, however, our spirit may still be wary and uncertain – it may have been taught never to pull that lever on the far right or told to flick the same switch every time it comes across a problem in life. It may even have been told never to eat the fruit from the tree in the middle of the garden..."

We were less than 40 meters from the leader when he stopped once more and turned towards us. Wildebeest are definitely not the prettiest of animals: with menacing horns, a dark scruffy mane, a fringe of long black hair down the throat and a black face that looks something between a buffalo and a bison, they are ugly. The leader looked worse. He was big, probably weighing in excess of 275 kilograms or 600 pounds, and judging from all the marks on his body, he had been in many fights. I noticed that his left eye was blind.

"Meet Scar-face," Teecha said. "I have to talk to him. Come along but stay behind me."

All the animals behind Scar-face had stopped in line as far back as 100 meters. They stared at us silently while shaking their heads every now and then. Further back the rest of the herd continued onwards, and as the individual animals realized something was happening, they also stopped, slowly forming a formidable audience. There was a strong scent in the air and all of a sudden the small pestering Kalahari flies appeared. Trying to keep them away from my face, I stayed behind Teecha as he walked towards the animal.

We were about 20 meters from Scar-face when he slowly started to walk towards us. Teecha told me to stop and wait. It was difficult to believe what I saw next. The animal recognized Teecha, came straight towards him and rose onto his hind legs twice, before nudging and licking him, less than ten meters from me. I felt like sitting down because my legs gave way. Teecha patted the animal on his neck and talked to him. I heard him clearly but I couldn't understand a word. Scar-face obviously did, for he shook his head from time to time, as if agreeing about something and sometimes differing in opinion. Teecha pointed to me once and I felt silly when the wildebeest turned his one good eye in my direction. Standing with his back to me, Teecha gestured towards the north and then pointed south. After another few seconds he patted the animal again, turned round and walked back to me.

Speechless, I watched in wonder as Scar-face turned and purposefully walked back towards the herd. As he did so, the animals nearby also turned around. In less than a minute, as if obeying an unspoken command, the whole herd changed direction and then slowly walked south, grazing calmly as they did. I glanced at Teecha who looked very satisfied with himself.

"Let's go back, Ace, it's getting late."

I stood up slowly.

"I don't believe this, Teecha, you changed their mind – how did you do it? Why?"

"I didn't Ace, they did. I explained to Scar-face that if he carried on in that direction he would lead his herd to mass suicide. In dry times like now many animals migrate to lake *Ngami* and lake *Xau*, northeast from here. They've been doing so for thousands of years but now they can't get there anymore. Should they try to do it, they end up against the veterinary cordon fences put up for no reason other than man's greed. There they would die in their thousands, just before reaching the water and better pastures. It has happened many times. I told him not to worry and to stay around here because it will rain."

"Yes, I know about those fences – it's terrible – but how did you..."

"Ace, I told you there are many things in minds, but it seems like humans have lost most of the basics to understand it. Imagination is one of the things you really need."

He was about to exercise my imagination.

"You are the captain of a sophisticated spaceship, Pheon 1. You're sitting at the main control panel. In front of you are rows of buttons, flickering lights, gauges, TV screens, levers and displays from on-board computers. The computers are programmed to handle many situations automatically and to constantly feed you with information as to where you are and what is happening. They control and monitor most of the ship's bio-systems. You're wearing a spacesuit and special helmet with built-in earphones and a microphone system to communicate with your subordinates and with ground control. Pheon 1 is the product of the latest technology, and though you have commanded similar ships before, you are excited and eager to see what she can do and what you can achieve with her. You are full of memories of what it is like to be out here in space.

You know what dangers to expect and how to cope with them and you have been thoroughly trained to handle any conceivable situation. Having set the Pheon on course to a remote part of your galaxy, she swiftly arrows through space close to light speed, at 0,9 'c'. You lean back and relax. Your mission is to assess and investigate other life forms and to relay the information back to Earth. Knowing that you are in full control of this fantastic ship fills you with mixed emotions. From the deep realms of your thoughts rise feelings of pride, achievement, happiness, expectation and adventure, yet mixed with uncertainty and unease, not knowing exactly what you may come across or what you may experience...

"OK Ace, before we turn your voyage of imagination into science fiction, let's use it as an analogy to come to grips with the mind. You, captain of the Pheon, are the spirit. The Pheon itself is your body or organism. It is equipped with fantastic sensors, radar scanners and other recording units, which instantly transmit situations and conditions to you. The control panel, linked to various other systems and computers, is your brain. You are able to make split second decisions and being properly trained, you press the right buttons or pull the right levers most of the time. You control the direction of the ship and you can set it on any course of your choice. You also have many automatic and manual defense mechanisms available to use whenever necessary at your own discretion.

"This action where you control the ship and decide what to do in any situation, is what you term the conscious or 'creative' mind: It is your choice, your decision, your mistake, based on information which you receive through your brain, which is the control panel, and correlated with your own experiences or memory. Your creative mind is the directing force, which decides on specific actions (after evaluation, perception and association), based on all available criteria, and as you'll see, memory plays an important role. Your creative mind is directly linked to your body through your physical senses like sight, hearing and touch. In fact, your conscious creative mind is your spirit, your soul, your own self...

"You also have a 'subconscious' mind – those on-board computers that control the automated functions of your spaceship without you having to worry about them, unless of course, something goes wrong and the conscious mind has to take control. The subconscious mind records and stores as much information as the conscious mind tells it to or programs it to do. It controls everything that the conscious mind allows it to or expects it to control. This fact is extremely important in your daily life.

"There is one especially powerful tool on your spaceship: it is called the 'creative subconscious' mind. This mind is like those on-board computers programmed to solve many problems and to suggest what action you should take in any given situation. Knowing that the creative subconscious mind is usually right, you blindly follow those suggestions – after all, you have programmed some of those computers yourself... Furthermore, it maintains all the ship's systems and it controls its drive and energy forces.

"The combined power of the subconscious- and creative subconscious minds is termed the 'subjective' mind. Now, when your subjective mind suggests an action that the creative conscious mind finds difficult to agree with, you have a problem – now **you** have to make the decision! It is here where another factor has to be considered: collective consciousness, when advice is required from ground control.

"What this means is that you could not have been on this mission if it wasn't for all the other spirits that made it possible. It is a joint venture made possible by all of mankind and Life itself.

"Something like the Pheon could never exist if it were not for the collective efforts, visions, emotions and in particular, the imagination of all concerned. There are many examples of this collective consciousness in nature. Take African termites – every single ant acts on behalf of and for the whole colony, to the extent that the colony becomes a physical organism which acts on behalf of and to the benefit of each individual ant. In that way the colony becomes a living force more powerful than the sum of the capabilities of each ant...

"It is the same thing that you see with migrating birds. On one specific day, millions of a certain species will flock together. Then, as if by common agreement, the whole 'organism' stirs, darkening the sky, as a journey across continents begins. This still happens in parts of the world, Ace – you were fortunate seeing all those wildebeest this afternoon. I wonder for how long you'll be able to see something like that."

Teecha's last words sounded sad. I glanced at him sideways and noticed that he wiped some dust from his eyes. It was dusty so I wiped mine too. Deep in thought about the wildebeest, and especially about the talk between Teecha and Scar-face, I couldn't think of much to say. We were still far from camp. Thirsty, I drank a few mouthfuls of water and handed the water bottle to Teecha.

"Thanks."

"I'm sure we'll still see it for many years to come, Teecha. From what you've told me I now realize that there is a collective consciousness rising from within mankind, to respect and to protect all life. People are more concerned."

"Eheh – and with man this collective consciousness could be frighteningly powerful. Consider for instance how certain individuals throughout the ages have influenced the minds of the masses, leading nations to empires and thoughts to ideologies that changed your world."

"Teecha, how come you know Scar-face and how did you communicate with him?"

By then I was used to his indirect answers: "There are more minds, Ace. Every spirit has an 'unconscious' mind. It is usually the black sheep amongst the different minds insofar as it contains material that has been repressed by the conscious. This material is mostly things like bad experiences in childhood when the 'young' spirit is very impressionable. Those experiences are filed away as far as possible. Unfortunately the creative mind is influenced by this unconscious knowledge, memories or experiences, which then have detrimental effects on an individual's life. Because the conscious mind does not want to know about those things, they are the reason an individual denies himself the full knowledge of himself. However, regression could be used to uncover traumatic experiences, with or without hypnosis. Once an individual 'knows' the cause of some or other phobia he has, he is often able to rid himself of it.

"Collective unconscious is something else to reckon with. It is basically the inherent character trait or archetype of a person, and is those experiences and knowledge gained from being human, within a certain culture, speaking that mother tongue, belonging to a specific religion or growing up in a certain part of the world. All species have a unique character and every culture has its own peculiarities. 'Typical French' you often say, or 'Only mad dogs and Englishmen go out in the midday sun'. Beings from outer space will probably refer to mankind as 'endangered earthlings'...

"Another influence on your characters could well be those mind boggling celestial objects we talked about: There is certainly enough scientific evidence and collective interest forcing you to seriously consider some claims of astrology. The fact that you are born within specific astrological ages under the influence of certain stars and planets, does seem to have definite effects on your minds and even your physical bodies. One example is the menstrual cycle of women occurring on average every 28 days, the same interval of time as that between the phases of the moon. Collectively, the minds of Pisces people function a little different than those of Aquarians, sometimes very differently. However, astrology has little to do with your future, Ace – that you determine yourself."

"Are you saying that I control my own future?" "Eheh, but we'll get to that. There is one more mind to mention, the all-important Universal Mind. This mind is your link with the metaconscious state. You are all aware of one another, of all other spirits and of the Ultimate Spirit. Your conscience, super-senses, instincts, knowledge of good and evil, and your desire to be, are parts of this mind. You are free to draw any information from it and to communicate with and through it at any time, as you have direct access to it. I used this mind to talk to Scar-face. If you're really sincere and absolutely truthful about something, there is no greater power. Most people know this – why else do they pray? But prayer should never be abused – forget about using it for your own greed or benefit and don't make a habit of it. Pompous rituals, fancy words and rhymes not from the heart have no effect."

The surroundings became familiar and I realized that we were close to camp. It was almost dark. We walked the last few minutes in silence, while I did battle with many thoughts. I was tired, thirsty, hungry and worried about the fact that I had already stayed longer than I'd intended. Teecha started picking up firewood and I followed his example. Arriving at camp, I dumped the bundle and flopped into my chair. Then I almost jumped up again – Xi'tau shook his head and complained loudly from underneath the umbrella thorn, as if questioning our whereabouts. My first shock made way for something else, though. I could have sworn that he looked pleased to see us and I felt like giving him a hug. However, I wasn't sure if he would have appreciated it – almost like the feeling when you do not know whether you should take hold of the hand of your first love or not.

"Where has he been all day?" I asked.

"Oh, he's very lazy, especially after eating – probably been sleeping off his full belly."

Teecha fiddled with the kettle, scratched open hot coals from the ashes and revived the fire in seconds. I got the hint and was about to get up to make supper when he said:

"Ace, before your Pheon gets outside radio contact, let's use it for another example. Consider what may happen when some connections between one of the main computers and the control panel are damaged. Although the computer may still function properly on its own, you, the spirit, no longer receive the information it supplies you with and you may be totally unaware of what is happening. You cannot process data or store anything in your memory banks because you do not receive it. Your ship is suffering 'brain damage', yet there is absolutely nothing wrong with you. In fact, nothing can ever go wrong with you.

"By now you should be getting the picture of what the mind really is. All those interactions between a spirit, its body, its various minds, the environment and all other spirits, **is** 'the mind'.

"The spirit's memories of its experiences and its knowledge or wisdom, are part of the spirit itself and also part of the Ultimate Spirit. A body or organism is necessary to provide experiences and knowledge and once it has fulfilled that need, is no longer required. There is a very good reason for any physical body to be mortal. If a spirit couldn't get rid of its body at some stage, life may become extremely boring – would you like driving the same car or wearing the same clothes throughout this life?

"If you stay I'll show you how powerful the mind actually is and what basic truths have already been taught through the ages. And Ace, I'm sure you'll find it interesting to discover that modern man, with all his 'Pheons', is merely rediscovering the meaning of life..."

******

'Our normal waking consciousness, rational consciousness as we call it, is but one special type of consciousness, while all about it, parted by the filmiest of screens, there lie potential forms of consciousness entirely different.

We may go through life without suspecting their existence, but apply the requisite stimulus, and at a touch they are there in all there completeness...'

William James, American philosopher and psychologist

******

THE FIFTH DAY

Vultures were circling the a kilometer ahead of us. I was in two minds about whether to see what the vultures were up to or to continue tracking the spoor we were following. About an hour ago, we had come across the fresh tracks of a leopard. The previous night Teecha had promised to show me the spoor of various animals and how to track them down. We had been following the tracks of a small herd of oryx since early morning when he spotted those of the big cat.

His knowledge of animals and their habits was remarkable. In a low voice, he would tell me exactly what kind of animal made the spoor, how many they were, how long ago the spoor was left, what they were doing and what they were up to.

Xi'tau followed us rather unwillingly, closer than before but still keeping his distance at about 50 meters. I was eager to track the leopard, although Teecha had warned that it was Half-tail, and that he was a mean one.

"How do you know that this is Half-tail and why do you call him that?"

"You see this spoor from his left hind paw? It has only two toes. He was once caught in a trap by his tail and, fortunately for him, he was trapped only by the toes of his hind paw. He managed to rip his paw out of the trap, but had to bite and chew his own tail off to free himself..."

"That's horrible, Teecha." With a shiver I asked: "Who had set the trap?"

"White hunters who wanted his skin for their ladies' fur coats."

He pointed out some eland tracks and then explained how he knew that they were left about three days ago:

"There are many things telling you that, like the dryness of their droppings or urine, how the sand blew over the tracks, if you can remember in what direction and how strong the wind was, and to what extent grass stems and broken twigs recovered afterwards. You also look at the fresh tracks left by the many small and other larger nocturnal animals like springhare and compare them to the other."

I recognized some old wildebeest spoor and was reminded of something.

"Teecha, you still haven't told me how you came to know Scar-face?"

"Eheh. It was during a cold and dry winter, a long time ago. I was hunting many days south from here when I heard what sounded like a terrible fight – loud growling accompanied by the sorry bellowing of an animal in distress. I ran closer and found that a leopard had attacked a young wildebeest. Somehow the wildebeest had managed to survive the first attack and to shove his whole body backwards into a thicket of blade thorn. There was no way for the leopard to get to his prey and the wildebeest courageously fought him off with his horns. I decided to chase the leopard away and then to kill the wildebeest as it would have saved me the effort of three more days of hunting. It is possible to chase even lions away from their prey – most animals are instinctively afraid of humans and if you put up a good show, they'll back off. I ran towards the leopard, shouting and screaming and throwing stones and pieces of wood at him. At first he made a stand for it but when I screamed louder and ran towards him with my spears, his nerve went before mine did and he retreated, the disgust on his face more disturbing than his display of strength.

"Making sure that he stuck to his decision, I turned to the wildebeest. His whole body was covered with blood from the blade thorns and from the scratch marks over his back where the leopard's claws had missed their grip. His left eye was ripped out, probably during the ensuing fight from the bush. I raised my spear to finish him off. He turned his head to the left, exposing his neck but looked at me beseechingly with one eye. I couldn't kill him. I must have stood like that with my raised spear for a few minutes, until I slowly dropped it and walked away. He crawled out of the bush and followed. That night he was still with me. It was very strange so I threw my bones. N!odima told me to patch up his eye and to clean his wounds. For days he stayed with me until one morning I woke up and found he had left. I could have tracked him down but decided not to, and never saw him again till yesterday."

The excitement of following a leopard on foot without any weapon had released a fair amount of adrenaline into my bloodstream. The fact that a large Kalahari lion followed us all the time didn't cross my mind. I became wary of everything around me and jerked with fright as a black korhaan cock flew up from under my feet, loudly squawking 'Krrraqr!... krrraqr!...' He flew away speedily, complaining coarsely all the time. Just when I thought he was going to land, he suddenly flew straight up in the air, somersaulted twice and then slowly glided almost vertically down, his wings acting like a parachute and both legs held out straight in front like the landing gear of some fancy airplane. He kept cursing us until he landed. My sense of awareness then more acute, I was able to spot the spoor clearly three or four meters ahead. Teecha also got excited and he reminded me to speak and walk quietly.

"Look!" he pointed with a whisper, "here he scratched his nails," and a little later, "here he urinated to mark his territory. He is close-by..."

Teecha climbed onto the top of a termite mound for a better view. In my eagerness to find the leopard I continued on the spoor. About 25 meters further on I lost it and started walking in a small outgoing spiral, as he had told me to do whenever one loses the trail. All the time I stared intently at the ground trying to find the tracks again. What happened next happened so quickly that I only have memories of certain vivid scenes.

As I stepped near the entrance of an old ant bear hole, a snarling leopard shot out of it. The shock and fear I experienced is difficult to describe but was enough to render me motionless. Half-tail leapt away for ten or so meters but suddenly stopped and turned back. He must have thought I was going to be easy prey. I was barely over the first shock when I sensed the danger of the new situation. I didn't have time to even think of putting up a show. The leopard flattened his ears, sank down on his belly and I remember a loud whistle, as half a tail swished left and right. He purposefully came a step or two closer, with black slits in hateful eyes. Then he charged, yellow and black, low over the ground...

“Shiiiiiit!” said my spirit, for my voice couldn’t speak.

From the left came a low, grumbling roar. A streak of brown-black hair caught the corner of my eyes, now fixed on the leopard. The next instant Xi’tau thudded into the side of Half-tail, barely a few feet in front of me. A terrible scramble ensued, accompanied by vicious growls, clawing nails and bared fangs.

Fortunately for me, the leopard was no match for Xi’tau, who gave him a good whack on the rear before Half-tail sped off into the bush, limping slightly. Xi’tau didn’t pursue him but turned round to me and then calmly lay down, looking pleased with himself. He started to lick his left thigh, which was trickling blood. Half-tail had left his mark...

Dust hanging in the air, my legs decided they’d had more than enough once again, and I sat down carefully, fumbling for my cigarettes. “Ace, you really should be more careful – you’re in the Kalahari, my friend – and you smoke too much!” I couldn’t answer him and neither could my trembling fingers get hold of a cigarette. I kept staring at Xi’tau.

An hour or so later we came upon the place where Xi’tau had killed the springbok. By then I had calmed down but I didn’t listen to what Teecha had to say on the way. He carried on as if nothing had happened. Needless to say, I had lost all my fear of Xi’tau. Both he and I seemed to sense something as he now followed us closely, like a big dog. I longed to touch him.

A few vultures flew away from what was left of the kill. Like undertakers overseeing the last remains, three marabou storks watched us from a safe distance.

Xi’tau sniffed around and then playfully pawed one of the remaining bones, which were scattered all over the place. Flies and maggots crawled through the skull.

“Amazing,” I thought, “there’s hardly a piece of skin left.”

Commando ants scrambled over the sand just in case a scrap or two had been left for them.

“The death of one is the bread of another,” I decided. The stench was unbearable and we moved to the shade of a nearby tree, upwind from the carrion. We sat down and I stared at the leftover carcass. Confused by many mixed emotions, I remarked:

"Yes, life **is** a bitch – and then you die..."

Teecha mumbled something about understanding life and referred to some book, but I wasn't listening to him. All I did was to weigh up life against death in my mind. He answered my thoughts:

"It's the Balance."

"Yes Teecha, I suppose there is this thing called balance, but what is it and why is it necessary?"

******

THE BALANCE

And the Firmament has He
Raised high, and He has set up
The Balance..."

The Qur'an, Sura LV : 7

"As defined in most dictionaries, Ace, balance means the condition of equilibrium between two forces, or a state of rest or poise between equal but opposing forces. The words 'forces' or 'powers' are always used to explain this condition. If something does not balance or should anything go out of balance, you end up with a problem. You talk about the balance of power (politically), the economic balance (supply and demand), the ecological balance (that's life and death if you will) and about many more things or aspects that supposedly have to balance.

"Humans have an uncanny sense of knowing when something is out of balance. You are quick to say: 'Too much of this or too little of that'. You use the adverb 'too', to express something excessive, inadequate or out of line with your perception of what it should be at that instant to be in balance. In fact, anything that you attach the word 'too' to, is no good. When you say 'too good', you mean too much of a good thing – which is very different from good. Anyway, you know instinctively when something like a situation, a time or an emotion is out of balance. Most of you will do anything and use everything in your power to put such a condition back in line with your belief of the balance it should have. And if you can't sort it out you'll go to extremes such as war, killing each other and many other things in the process."

Teecha's tone of voice had changed. He was serious and agitated. My question about balance must have touched something. I thought it best to remain silent.

"Good examples of an imbalance are your world wars, the Gulf war, the wars in Korea and Bosnia and spates of violence across the entire earth. Something stepped out of line. Whether it is the balance of power, the balance of oil prices, the balance of man's perception between good and evil or the balance of human rights, it doesn't seem to matter. Like most other times in the past, you yourself caused the imbalance, giving you a reason to destroy each other. That's your own problem, but in the process you upset other things that are in balance, until the graph of life reaches an all time low. Apart from completely innocent people that your bombs destroy or maim, those same bombs wipe out many other innocent life forms. Each exploding bomb, whether it hits its target or not, kills thousands of living creatures. Every oil-slick, every smoking pillar of soot, kills. Experiments with nuclear and other weapons in the remotest parts of the sea or in 'uninhabited' desert regions, kill many thousands of living creatures.

"Ace, for those of you who think deserts are desolate and of no use to life, think again. They support the most intricately balanced life forms on Earth, some primitive, some highly advanced. Deserts, whether consisting of rock and sand or vast areas of ice and snow, to the deepest and remotest oceans, teem with life. They're considered to be the origin of life – biologists and scientists try to create life by simulating the environmental conditions of deserts. The most primitive forms of life and the longest living are to be found there. To date you're still waiting for that sporting spirit to side itself with your efforts at creating life.

"With foolish, destructive, senseless wars and political squabbles, homo sapiens seems to be set on destroying himself and everything else. Mass murder is something nature does not tolerate, especially when man's war games and technological advances interfere with the balance of life. She may decide to shock man back to his senses or to wipe him out. So far she's been patient, as every human being acts as a host to something like one million other living organisms, whether he likes it or not.

"Man is just another species on Spaceship Earth. Other beings, or for that matter living 'matter', outweigh mankind literally and figuratively. There are, for instance, something like thirty million species of insects on Earth. The estimated number of living insects amounts to 1,000,000,000,000,000 – a thousand million million. Their total physical mass of about a million million kilograms, exceeds all that of mankind.

"And, Ace, man is but one species of more than a million classified animals on earth, all the living creatures like mammals, birds, reptiles, insects and the fish you know about, let alone plants. You are genuinely outnumbered. Nature will not continue to be patient with man as she can do very well without you. Consider this: Should mankind disappear from Earth, no more than three insect species would be adversely affected: they are human lice which will no doubt, try their luck with baboons or gorillas. Without man, nature would revert to her former state of equilibrium within 10,000 years, with no further loss of more species except through natural disasters, apart from those which you have brought to the verge of extinction. On the other hand, should all insects disappear from earth, life as you know it would be doomed – their loss would affect every other living thing. No Earth life could survive that, yet none would be bereaved by the loss of man."

Leaving me to consider this insignificance, he continued:

"In Greek mythology, Gaia is the Earth Mother goddess, the great provider and nourisher. Without her, humans, animals and plants could not live. Even today, Gaia is acknowledged as the notion that all living things on earth interact as one super-organism, a web of life. Gaia can't stand anything to be out of balance any more than you can. It is said that because she cares for all life, she will protect man. She won't. Her patience with man is running out. Being life itself she will look after all the inter related life forms of plants and animals supported by the Earth."

"You make it sound as though we're doomed, Teecha. Surely that's not all there is to it?" I objected. "Like every other living being, you and I and all men have a right to be here – we are all children of the universe. There must be something we can do – things can't be that bad."

"Eheh, Ace, but seeing that you consider yourselves the most intelligent and wisest species on Earth, you have a responsibility. Your right to be doesn't give you the right to destroy. You are able to understand what the balance is all about and to assist in maintaining it. If you don't, your own chance of a higher level of beingness is small. The Ultimate Spirit is Life and loves all Life. Do you think there could be a heaven for those who care nothing about and blatantly destroy life?"

"No, it wouldn't be right... I think –"

"Tchi... tchi... Aowa, Ace, not 'think' – you **know** it doesn't work like that. What you should think about is what this balance really entails."

"But that's what I asked you in the first place."

"Eheh – and you've just answered it yourself."

My disconcerted emotions must have ended up as an expression. I'm quite sure that the fleeting smile I noticed on Teecha's lips had something to do with my face. When he continued in his normal manner, I felt a little better.

"Ace, because of your sense of balance, you use many different words for things you consider to be 'opposites'. For instance, you are exceptionally good at describing opposing conditions and emotions with words like love versus hate, happy versus miserable, 'on top of the world' versus 'down in the dumps', excited versus bored, war versus peace, beautiful versus ugly, good versus evil, god versus devil. In fact, you have words and phrases to express just about everything you 'comprehend' or find 'incomprehensible'. By the way, note the spelling of your words for 'good', 'god', and 'evil', 'devil'. Anyway, we've already talked about certain aspects of the solar system, your own galaxy and the universe, which are in balance. By now you know that:

there is something and there is nothing;

there are forces attracting matter and forces repelling it;

there is life and there is death;

there is order and there is chaos;

there is light and there is darkness;

and, there is 'no beginning' and 'no end'...

There are many other things in balance: "Although you may be familiar with the tale of Adam and Eve, let's look at a few statements in the story more closely. Take for instance, Genesis 3 verses 2 to 6:

'We may eat from the trees in the garden, but God did say, "You must not eat fruit from the tree that is in the middle of the garden, and you must not touch it, or you will die." "You will not surely die," the serpent said to the woman... "For God knows that when you eat of it your eyes will be opened, and you will be like God, knowing good and evil"... When the woman saw that the fruit of the tree was good for food and pleasing to the eye, and also desirable for gaining wisdom, she took some and ate it.'

"Note, Ace, that those words come from the New International Version of The Disciple's Bible. Other versions and translations, like that of the King James version states: '...ye shall be as gods, knowing good and evil.' Your interpretation of the actual meaning of a passage becomes difficult because of all your different translations, which change the meaning drastically."

Teecha emphasized some of the words he quoted very dramatically. We had been walking for quite a while and I felt hot and sticky. The air felt humid and I must have been doing a good bit of woolgathering. Thinking that he was being a little too serious, I remarked: "Yes, and to think that all our troubles started with an apple."

He stopped dead, turned around with flashing eyes and looked me straight in the face: "You may think it's funny and irrelevant, Ace, but it's time you disregarded all the nonsense you were led to believe. The tale also shows that women have a much bolder spirit than men, as Eve, the Mother or female spirit of all mankind, took that chance to gain wisdom, rather than that negative interpretation of 'original sin' you all attach to it."

Shaking his spears, he walked off with another escapade:

"You talk about 'Mother Earth' and you pray to 'Our Father who art in Heaven'. You assume the Ultimate Spirit to be male and attach male characteristics to 'Him', like almighty, powerful, lord, king, awesome, rock, strength, avenging. Those adjectives all come from your Bible. What about the female characteristics of love, faithfulness, wiping away tears, forgiveness, kindness, tenderness and care? Those adjectives describing God are also from the Bible. You say: 'Behind every great man is a great woman...' If the Ultimate Spirit is a male, then who's behind Him?

"Your society's male chauvinists may not like this, but the original meaning of the name Adam denotes both male and female. You should know this, Ace, for in your Afrikaans language, consisting of many words borrowed from all over Europe and from Africa's peoples, the word to indicate mankind is 'Mens'. Mens does not distinguish between male and female. Anyway, if it wasn't for Eve all men would still be in paradise, totally ignorant of life and half the whole."

I thought about something but before commenting, he outwitted me:

"Eheh, you're quite right Ace – who would have cared?"

Scenes flashed through my mind – a shaking rattle in front of a baby's face... Interesting noise, beautiful colors, clever movements that keep it out of reach, like a lure to the reality of knowing. There is truly something out there, if only I could touch it, smell it, chew on it. Small clumsy fingers groping... Now what happened? It's gone.

"There's no such thing as something for nothing, Ace, except for one thing, which you all seem to waste. Anyway, you may well debate and interpret certain statements and parables in the Qur'an, the Bible and other holy scriptures metaphorically, yet the truth spoken in Genesis 3 is rather literal. Once a spirit reaches man's – or mens' – level of existence it knows the difference between good and evil. Whether this came about through eating that proverbial apple or not is irrelevant – being a human spirit you just know it. Animals, so you believe, do not have that knowledge – even those that can be trained. You all think animals do not know about good and evil, except to know what pleases or displeases the master. You should reconsider that…

"Even plants are more intelligent than you think. Experiments have shown that plants experience emotions such as fear and love. Because you don't like the findings, you create enough controversy on the reliability of the results to put mankind back on his arrogant pedestal. Yet according to the facts of your own branch of science, palaeontology, plant spirits have been on this planet longer than any other form of life. Is there any reason then why they shouldn't be highly intelligent?"

I just had to reply. "Teecha, we move around and they don't. We cultivate them, look after them and we eat them. Agreed, we are dependant on them for our own survival, but they are all dumb life forms, why else do we call senseless humans a 'vegetable'?"

After his answer that day I will always view plants in a different light.

"Ace, look at the way plants reproduce their species, using most other life forms like insects, fish, birds, mammals and man. Look at their seeds, some aerodynamically shaped to benefit from wind and air turbulences or designed to float for months in sea currents, to eventually root on a remote island or distant continent. Should man ever travel to other planets or to the stars, he may well be sowing the spores of plants like ferns all over the universe. Spores will be hiding in his clothes, shoes, nostrils and intestines – a good sneeze or relieving yourself is likely to establish a fern or some other plant. Plants are indeed cunning, and they may well be using humans to cultivate them, care for them and to distribute them around the world. You love your beautiful flower gardens, plants and fields of wheat and corn. What do you use to brew your liquid spirits and where do tobacco and most other drugs come from? You even distinguish between good plants and evil ones, labeling some beneficial and others weeds.

"You stumble across unknown facts every so often: A number of kudu were kept in a quarantine area on a game farm. The confined area had more than enough food for the kudu in the form of mopane trees, which as you know, are a natural source of food for game and livestock. Even the dry leaves are highly nutritious. After being in the quarantine area for a few days, the kudu stopped grazing the mopane leaves and started to starve. At first it was thought that they had contracted a disease but nothing could be diagnosed. Stress, often a problem with captured game, was ruled out. Game wardens and veterinary surgeons alike were all baffled.

"It was only when somebody noticed that the kudu moved from one tree to the next, trying to eat the leaves but each time almost spitting them out, that a strange but logical discovery was made: Being in the confined area the kudu had to graze more on each individual tree than they normally do in the wild. After chemical tests it was found that the leaves were totally inedible, containing a substance which made them extremely bitter. Leaves of trees outside the area tested normal. The balance inside had been disturbed, causing the trees to defend themselves by giving off the bitter substance. In the wild, grazing animals never eat all the leaves from one tree or shrub. As an animal starts grazing, most plants soon release an acrid substance in their leaves which causes the animal to move on. Quite clever, Ace, for dumb vegetables to force this balance. If man persists in destroying the rainforests, who knows what they might come up with?"

He glanced at me with a wink. That served to darken my mood, which had slowly changed to something bordering on melancholy. I felt disappointed in my own lack of knowledge and in mankind's insolence. I wondered why there is so much ill-fortune and misery in the world and couldn't figure out any purpose for it all. Teecha stooped down to look at a few busy termites, then walked on silently, leaving me with my thoughts. Eventually I tried to share my distress and waved my hand across the land.

"Teecha, surely all this could be different – or better than it is. Why can't life just be nice? Why all this... this badness?" "Eheh, it could be better, Ace, for you, if you change your thinking and your attitude. Maybe you'll do that someday. But first, let's steal an egg." He had stopped and stared ahead, with the palm of his left hand turned backwards gesturing me to stop. I stumbled straight into him.

"What?"

"Shhh ..." With his spears in his right hand, he pointed to a male ostrich staring straight back at us about 150 meters ahead.

"He's alone," I whispered. "What's this about an egg?"

"There, close to the three small rain trees – she's lying on the nest."

I saw the trees but it took me the best part of a minute to see the female. It also took a good bit of spear-pointing and explanation from Teecha. When I finally saw her, I remembered what he had told me about looking for shapes and not colors – her dull plumage blended in completely with the surroundings, in sharp contrast to the male's bright black and white feathers. The male bird remained motionless but even from that distance, his large rounded eyes spelled discontent.

"OK Ace, here's what we'll do: Xi'tau and I will walk straight to the nest. As soon as the female sees us walking towards her she'll get up and run away to try and distract us. You must follow about 50 meters behind us and fix your eyes on the spot from where she gets up. Once she gets up, Xi'tau and I will run closer to the nest. When the male figures out that we're going towards the nest, he'll try to chase us away and so will she. We will run away to the right and being silly birds, they'll follow us. We'll keep them occupied while you run to the nest and steal an egg, but you must take one only if there are less than seven or eight eggs in the nest. If there are more, leave them and run away from us to the left. Should anything go wrong and either of the birds start chasing you, hide inside some shrubs or fall down and lie face down."

"Teecha, those birds are much bigger and faster than us, and they can kick a man to pieces. I don't think this is a good idea."

"Ace, I told you they are silly – if they run at speed they can't turn quickly, and because they only kick forward and down, not forward and up, they can't really get at you when you're lying down. Besides, they quickly lose interest once they think you're dead."

"Thanks, that's very comforting to know – and why must I only take an egg if there are eight or less? I'd feel much better to pinch one if there were more..."

"She lays between 12 and 15 eggs and then both she and the male start to incubate them, she during the day and he at night. The chicks all hatch within a day or two of each other. If you want a fresh egg then you must steal one before she has laid the whole batch." He gave three short whistles and Xi'tau eagerly trotted closer, like a dog waiting for a stick to be thrown. Still I wasn't impressed:

"Don't you think she's already laid all her eggs?"

"We'll soon find out."

Teecha walked on quickly and openly, straight towards the female. Xi'tau followed him expectantly, tail straight up in the air. I watched the action as if I was not going to be any part of it, until the female suddenly got up and ran towards the male. Teecha beckoned me to follow. As I started running I remembered that I had to fix my eyes on the spot she got up from. I tried my best and kept running. Already Teecha was more than 70 meters in front of me, with a twitching tail right behind him.

"You're going nuts," somebody said to me.

Just as Teecha predicted, the male came running towards them with a gaping beak, opened wings and fluffed out feathers, which made him look twice his size. Xi'tau ran past Teecha and swerved to the right. The ostrich boldly chased after Xi'tau for a few meters but then changed his mind and went for Teecha, who had also started running to the right. He still had the time to gesture at me to run on. The female was also going for Teecha. Worried out of my mind, I almost stopped running but then noticed that both the birds had turned onto Xi'tau again. He had run back to them and like a playful dog, teased them into attacking him, at the same time leading them away from where Teecha was.

Deciding to stick to the task in hand, I realized that I had run past the nest. Teecha was about 60 meters away pointing anxiously to my right. Turning back I saw the nest and ran towards it counting four... five... six... eggs. As I grabbed one, the female ostrich, who was then still occupied with Xi'tau, saw through the plan. A day in primary school flashed through my mind – my first try in a rugby match. I tucked the ball under my arm and ran.

Glancing back for support I saw Teecha trying to distract the female with waving hands and actually running towards her. It worked, and she forgot about me again. Still running for some imaginary goal post, I looked back again to see a rather confused ostrich hen but no Teecha. She was at least 75 meters away from me. Still further than that a very irate kick-boxing male ostrich was trying his best to deliver a fatal blow to an arch-enemy. At that stage his lady decided that he was quite able to handle himself and jogged over to her nest. Panting for breath, I took cover behind a sickle bush and wondered where Teecha was. She carefully inspected the remaining eggs with a long curved neck and I sincerely hoped she couldn't count.

The last I saw of the male ostrich was when he disappeared over a low dune in a cloud of dust, chasing the big lion. I can only imagine how that bird must have bragged that evening. Anyway, after counting and recounting, the female seemed satisfied that all her eggs were still there and lay down on the nest. Teecha appeared stooping low, about 100 meters to my right. He gestured that I should keep a low profile and to meet him further on, which I gladly agreed to do. I ran in the direction he pointed.

Within a minute or two he was next to me, and said smiling: "Ace, I see you've even mastered the art of running behind yourself. You would have made an excellent fly half – pity you didn't have that bird for a coach."

Still breathless, I handed him the egg and said proudly: "Your turn to make supper."

He put the egg into his skin bag and walked on in the direction of the camp, or so I assumed, for I had no clue where we were.

"Incidentally, Ace, ostrich cocks mate for life. Should the female die, the male will mourn her for the rest of his life and never take another wife. However, if the male dies the female will run off with the first available guy who shows an interest."

"Interesting – probably life's way to maintain the species... or the balance you were talking about."

"Eheh, and by the way, I don't see too much badness around here. Nature is always in complete balance unless humans come along and upset the applecart, which they are exceptionally good at. For the time being, we'll leave man out of the picture.

"Muse a little on the fact that all creatures on Earth, all plants, everything under the sea and in the air, all bacteria and even viruses, live and exist in perfect harmony, with themselves, their environment, the seasons that come and go and with all the forces acting upon them. These spirits pursue the experiences of their existence actively and accept, matter-of-factly, life and death on a daily basis. Life and death, or the attaching and detaching of spirits to organisms are also in perfect balance. There are never really 'too many' of this species or 'too little' of those – all exists in symbiosis and all are dependant on one another.

"This joint existence, nature or Gaia herself, is fantastically beautiful. You only need to appreciate the beauty of flowers and butterflies, colorful birds, landscapes, a flock of white egrets flying against black thunderclouds, starlit nights or young antelope joyfully playing on the plains after a spring shower.

"On the other hand, there is ugliness. Blood and disease, weeds and thorns, destruction after a storm or fire, pain and suffering, drought and famine, a young zebra strangled in a barbed wire fence or the despair of a baby animal who has lost its mother. Eheh, that is so. You find it difficult to accept this ugliness and you argue how a God of love, almighty and all that, can be so cruel? It says in Genesis 1:

'God saw all that he had made, and it was very good...'

"Not too good, not good enough, but very good – indeed, perfect. If you believe in an almighty God, then certainly He must be perfect and so is His creation. 'Perfection' cannot improve, and if at any time during eternity God's creation deteriorates, it was not perfect in the first place. It is still perfect and eternity still exists, so if man thinks that he will be allowed to change or disturb this eternal balance, he'll first have to think himself right out of creation. Can you think of a better way, Ace? If you were God, can you think of something you'd like to change without upsetting the balance? Maybe God should have kept man out of the picture too. If you do think of something, please let me know."

My mind turned blank. For a second I experienced what it must be like to be nonexistent, nothing. Then, in the next instant, the same feeling of a few days before: seeing life's secrets through the brilliance of a crystal-ball, it popped like a soap-bubble before sharing them. I realized straight away that a little seed was left, something I had to nurture and cultivate. But I also started to question my own balance.

"Stop worrying, Ace, and think about this: The whole universe is in balance – from the particles that make up matter to the forces controlling it, to the forces themselves. According to your own scientists, the most remarkable thing about the universe is that it is sitting on the borderline between expansion and collapse. The probabilities against it being on this border are enormous, yet it is so close that they haven't been able to decide on which side it's on.

"Nuclear physicists have discovered more delicate balances. If the strong nuclear force we discussed were just slightly weaker, no elements other than hydrogen could exist. If it were stronger then hydrogen, the most abundant element in the universe would not exist. If that was the case, stars and galaxies as you know them could not exist. If the force of gravity were stronger, most stars would be thousands of times smaller than they are. They would then exist for less than ten years, not even allowing man his 'three score years and ten' – let alone time for evolution. If the force of gravity were weaker or centrifugal forces were stronger than they are, then matter would probably not succumb to being pulled together, leaving space cold and devoid of light and life..."

Teecha remained silent for a while and I marveled at what he had said.

I thought that I was just coming to grips with the whole concept of balance when he remarked, rather casually:

"Even the Ultimate Spirit is in balance."

"Sorry, I wasn't here – what did you say?"

"You heard me the first time."

"How on earth did you work that one out?"

"Its simple, for there are two ultimate forces or powers, the Powers of Light and the Powers of Darkness, or as you know them, Good and Evil. These two opposing forces, one positive', one negative, are what make everything go round. One is happiness, the other misery, one is order, the other chaos, one is health, the other disease, one creates, the other destroys, one is Life, the other Death. What is more Ace, because both these forces exist within and as a part of eternity, one has no chance of ever overpowering or destroying the other."

A sledgehammer hit my mind and shattered it to pieces. Trying to put everything back in place, to find a counter argument, it groped at logic, reason, instinct, knowledge, truth, conscience, consciousness, religion. Finally I said: "Teecha, I find your last statement difficult to perceive and more difficult to accept – it is contrary to all I was led to believe."

"Is it Ace? Are you afraid of the truth?"

"No. No, I'm not – I believe in it."

"There is but one Ultimate Truth: Within eternity there is a perfect balance. Everything changes constantly but eternally everything remains the same. Neither God nor the Devil could ever change that balance – if either of them could, they still have eternity to do it in. This should not be so difficult to accept, Ace. There could never have been death and destruction if there hadn't been life and creation in the first place and vice versa. To really fathom that may require some serious thought, but right now, at this instant, everything is still in perfect balance, as it always was and always will be.

"Furthermore, Ace, we spirits are all a part of the Ultimate Spirit, but we exist on different levels of consciousness within it, thus we all contribute to a Spiritual Balance, wittingly or not."

Although his explanation made sense I was still reluctant to accept it, but some primeval instinct told me he had a point, so instead I queried: "Teecha, what do you mean by Spiritual Balance?"

He stopped, looked around and walked to the nearest clearing between the grass and shrubs. Taking the digging stick from his bag, he started to scratch a sizeable diagram on the sand. I watched with interest. Nothing made sense until he explained:

"Ace, this is the X-axis which shows the existence of spirits through their events or lifetimes. The Y-axis indicates the different planes of existence of spirits within the Ultimate Spirit. Above the X-axis is positive or Good, below is negative or Evil."

Then he drew a number of dotted horizontal lines.

"These lines above and below the X-axis are planes of existence, let's say levels 1 to 3 above, and minus-1 to minus-3 below."

He numbered each line separately. Then he carefully jotted a number of vertical lines, equally spaced.

"Each of these shows one life-event of a spirit's existence, let's call them events 1 to 4. Now take the existence of a spirit of lower intelligence than man," and he scratched a waving line along the X-axis.

"Because our chosen spirit does not yet know the difference between good and evil, and because its survival is based more on physiological needs than spiritual needs, it actively lives its first primitive event, moving through the ups and downs of lower levels.

"The same goes for a spirit of higher intelligence or when our first spirit reaches higher planes of existence, when during its second event, it may exist between levels 2 and minus-2. Still it is unaware of the fact that it is moving from good to evil and back. By now it may well be experiencing all sorts of emotions – self consciousness, love, fear, anger, feeling content with a full belly, association with its own kind and awareness of other spirits."

He scratched the mathematical symbol ∞ at the top and bottom of the

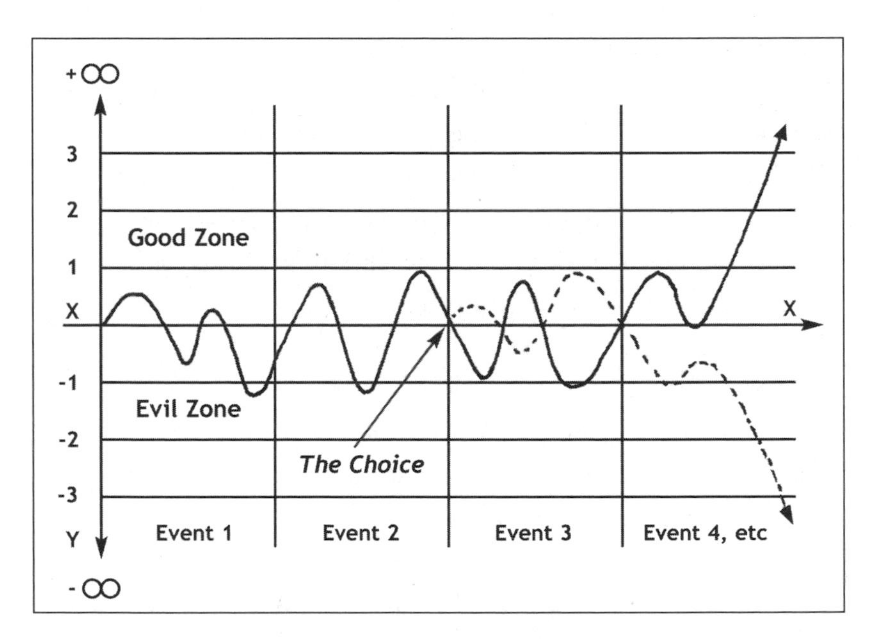

Figure 1: Spiritual Balance (Life)

Y-axis of his graph:

"Note, Ace, that the Y-axis extends to positive infinity and to negative infinity. There is an infinite number of levels either way, with an infinite number of spirits existing on all the different planes.

"It follows that at any instant this graph of life is always in perfect balance. This is the way it always was and always will be, the Ultimate design of eternity..."

As his words died away a strange spinning feeling of comprehension mixed with unreality took hold of me. It was so quiet and peaceful around us that it must have been a dream. Not even the whining sun beetles made their presence known. For a moment I saw the two of us discussing a picture on the sand and not far behind, a big but totally unconcerned lion. He looked a little tired. We were the only living beings in the middle of a great expanse. From high up above, my wings folded again and I spun back into myself. The dizzy feeling left me. I had forgotten about Xi'tau and glanced behind me to see him exactly where I had just seen him, and I wished that I could accept life the way he did.

"What you say makes sense, Teecha, but there are two things I don't understand. Firstly, where do all these spirits come from and how and why do they exist? Secondly, who or what decides on which side of the graph they will exist? To me it seems a little unfair not having any say in the matter."

"You'll soon know the answer to your first question. By the way, Ace, its nice to feel the wind beneath your wings, isn't it? To explain the second we'll single out one 'primitive' spirit. There he is – happily and contentedly going through his events, experiencing more each time, getting cleverer. All the time he stores his experiences and the knowledge he has gained in his memory, and he shares it with other spirits. Every now and then he extracts information from the collective consciousness and he often needs assistance from the Universal Mind. He becomes wiser...

"But he's in for the surprise of his lives. Once he reaches human levels of intelligence, let's say at the start of his third event right here on the graph, he is all of a sudden confronted with a choice he has never come across before. Up to now his choices to survive were merely to eat when hungry, drink when thirsty, rest when tired, fight or flee when in danger and to mate to reproduce. 'Now what the heck is this new choice between good and evil?' he wonders.

"The first thing he does is to wear the metaphorical fig leaves, which suggests that he is now torn from innocence and ignorance to self-consciousness, inter alia being able to distinguish between male and female. Fortunately or unfortunately, he knows just what this new knowledge means and he has to make a choice.

"During his next few life-events, he is very unsure of himself and stumbles back and forth between his choice of good and evil, either within the same event or in his next events. He desperately seeks help. Somehow he survives it and there comes the time when he finds himself more comfortable in the 'good' zone or in the 'evil' one. Once this happens, and once he moves to higher planes of existence within one of the two zones, it becomes exceedingly difficult to fall back to lower levels. Even more so, Ace, to cross the line between the zones. Our spirit is now basically good, or basically evil – and it was his own choice."

As he had done a few times that day, Teecha once more left me to my own thoughts and walked over to a termite mound. He scrutinized the ground around the insects' sand castle thoroughly, as if he were looking for something. We were close to camp. I was really tired. The sunset made an impression, though, I can still recall the beauty of that evening. I turned towards camp and walked on. Teecha remained at the termite mound and Xi'tau followed me. "Crazy," I thought: A few days ago I would have run for the nearest tree.

Still daydreaming and wondering when Xi'tau would be hungry again, my nerves nearly went when like a phantom, Teecha caught up with me and said from behind:

"Ace, a few more things about that positive zone: Once our spirit reaches higher planes, his primitive feelings and survival instincts become less important. Unfounded fears and worries disappear and he needn't concern himself with such emotions. He seems unaffected by troubles and misfortune that still control other spirits' events.

"He is able to pursue new experiences and to follow his dreams. He is aware of his spiritual existence and knows that he, his *'I'*, is immortal. His life becomes a challenge worth living as he tunes into existence itself, aware of the balance and understanding the most basic but at the same time, the highest principle of all..."

******

'Don't be afraid of misfortune,
and do not yearn after happiness:
it is, after all, all the same:
the bitter doesn't last forever,
and the sweet never fills the cup
to overflowing...'

Alexander Solzhenitsyn

******

THE SIXTH DAY

Back at camp after the Day of the Ostrich, Xi'tau decided to inspect the 4x4 vehicle more closely. He sniffed around it a few times, tried to bite the big off-road rubber tires, and finally came to the conclusion that the Landcruiser was his. With no further ado, he urinated onto the grill, then walked to the rear and squirted a few more times over the spare wheel and onto the contents in the back. After that it was truly his – anyone familiar with a domestic cat's habits should have no problem smelling out a lion's territory.

To emphasize his ownership, he paw-kicked some sand onto his trophy and then effortlessly jumped onto the bonnet, not realizing, of course, that the surface was smooth and not designed for lions weighing 120 pounds or 250 kilograms for lions who think in metric. Slipping, splitting and sliding, he clawed away to stay on top, leaving enough dents and scratch marks to baffle any insurance assessor. I closed my eyes and ears expecting the worst, but miraculously he had climbed onto the roof carrier by the time I looked again.

The extra foam mattresses and tents were right on top, covered with canvas. This bed was obviously more comfortable and warmer than the sand underneath the acacia, and he just flopped down. I thought about the camera on the vehicle's front seat and walked over to fetch it, but then decided not to push my luck.

Deciding not to challenge Xi'tau's ownership of the vehicle, I turned back to see what Teecha was doing. He was preparing a Kalahari mushroom omelet from the ostrich egg, which is the equivalent quantity of about two dozen hens' eggs. Catching the grin on his face, I queried: "And what's that smile about?"

The corners of his mouth widened but he busily carried on. I watched with interest as he managed to get the egg out of its shell through a little hole in the pointed end. The strong hard shell is never broken by the experienced Bushmen as it is used as a valuable container to hide water in the sand. Spilling some of the egg's contents, he mumbled something about my frying pan being too small, and that a tortoise skeleton in the coals would have worked much better.

Before dozing off that night I set my mind on getting up early. Proud of myself the next morning for getting my first chance to revive the fire and to catch Teecha still asleep, I offered him coffee in bed.

"Thanks, Ace," he said sleepily and raised himself from the sand. It was just getting light. He added: "You had a visitor just now. Here he is..."

Reaching for his bag, he proudly produced a thick but headless puff adder, over a meter long. The muscles in the snake's body were still twitching in the convulsions of death.

"He wanted to join you in the tent but turned into breakfast."

I shivered from two completely different thoughts and told him as tactfully as I could, that his omelet from the previous evening had been very filling and that it would last me at least the whole day. At the same time I started to wonder if he ever really slept. I had heard nothing until I woke up – surely he must have made some noise killing the snake, and how did he hear it or see it in the dark? If I had any appetite left, I slowly lost that too, watching him silently as he skinned and then fried a piece of the snake. Curiosity got the better of me, I decided to figure out his sleeping habits.

"Teecha, do you ever sleep?"

"Eheh, like a log – why do you ask?"

"Well, it seems to me that you never do. When I made coffee you looked fast asleep, how then did you see or hear the snake?"

"It's easy, Ace. I use my senses and some of the powers we all have. You did the same thing last night when you decided to get up early – you wanted to so you did."

"True," I thought. When setting an alarm if I need to rise early, I will usually wake a minute or two before it goes off.

"Yes, that's easy, but what about something like the snake?"

"Whether you're in the bush like the Kalahari or in a city like New York, there are certain things that you have to do and certain senses or instincts that you have to use in order to survive."

"Like?"

"They differ only in what you do, although you all use the same powers. I know that if I want to survive here, I have to be aware of everything that goes on around me, even while I'm asleep – I told you I am the bush. "Anyway, do you remember all those minds we spoke about?" I nodded. "Well, my subconscious is so conditioned and trained that it can sense danger while I'm fast asleep."

He must have thought that was a good enough explanation but I didn't. "Is that all?"

"Eheh, in the cities people have to use their subconscious and powers of intuition even more to survive, to sense when another driver is not going to stop or whether a financial deal is going to be profitable or not – a 'calculated risk' is usually no risk. But of course, Ace, people use those same powers in a negative way too, mostly to their own loss and detriment."

Pondering a little on his words, I remarked: "Teecha, you know many things and I know I've asked you this before, but where did you learn them and why are you here?"

I should have known by then that his answers could confuse me: "You should know that Ace – you came here looking for me, didn't you?"

"What do you mean?" I asked puzzled.

Sidestepping that too, he asked me: "Why are you here?"

"Well, I suppose because I drove into a hole and got stuck in the middle of nowhere and that fate or coincidence caused us to meet and all that. I didn't specifically come here to look for you."

"Then why did you take this route? And by the way, there's no such thing as fate. You arranged everything so that you could be here and you know that..."

"Now think before you speak again," I reminded myself, and then tried to put the facts together:

Fact 1: I came this way on impulse.

Fact 2: I wanted to see some Bushmen.

Fact 3: I accidentally drove into an ant bear hole.

Fact 4: The bees distracted me.

Fact 5: Our meeting was coincidental.

That familiar little voice on my shoulder said: "Liar!"

I started all over:

Fact 1: I wanted to come this way.

Fact 2: I needed someone to talk to.

Fact 3: I could have avoided the ant bear hole.

Fact 4: I lingered around on purpose.

Fact 5: I knew I was going to meet Teecha.

It was a long time before I spoke again:

"Teecha, I wish I could write a book about the things you've told me, but I wonder if anybody would believe me."

I said that without expecting any answer.

His reply confused me more: "But you've already written the book, Ace. Doesn't anybody believe you?"

All I could say was: "I haven't written any book. Are you being facetious?"

"*Aowa*... Can you just wish to eat when you're hungry or do you have to do something about it?"

"Teecha, what are you getting at?"

"*Tchi... tchi*... Ace, it seems as if you know little or nothing about one of your greatest gifts: Have you ever given some thought to the meaning of faith?"

******

THE POWER

'One mind goes left, the other right,
imagined by the spirit's goal.
The choice of darkness, or of light,
sets apart the eternal Whole.'

"Yes, Teecha, faith is something I'm supposed to have, but it doesn't work."

"Ace, many books and articles have been written about faith. Most of those writings try to tell you there is no limit to the power of the mind. That is absolutely true, but just as you have to learn to crawl and then to walk, so you have to learn what this power is and how to use it. You have a great problem when you do not know what faith really is, because then you unwittingly misuse or abuse it, with miserable effects to yourself and to others.

"The knowledge of what this power is and how to use it has been known to man since the dawn of civilization. It's nothing sinister, complicated or reserved for a select few – anyone can use it and you all do, daily, albeit mostly in a negative way and without realizing your true potential.

"The combined power of your spirit and your mind is unlimited. Unfortunately many of you do not know and sometimes do not want to know, the basics of this power. Like with most other things it simply exists. Nobody has ever come up with a new principle, physical law or scientific fact, but rather they've discovered how to use existing forces in the universe to their benefit.

"Who invented radar, electricity or gravity? Who ever dreamed 40 years ago, that today you would have calculators using light as the power source? Who would have thought merely 30 years back that a modern day fighter pilot uses his eyes to direct missiles to their target? Ace,

'... there is nothing new under the sun. Is there anything of which one can say, 'Look! This is something new'? It was here already, long ago;

it was here before our time.'
Ecclesiastes 1:9-10

"You should be grateful though, to thinkers like Alexander Graham Bell who 'discovered' the telephone. You should be even more grateful to people who rediscover the powers of the mind. But man tends to complicate things and that is exactly what you do with your second greatest gift. You over-complicate and eventually render useless a power that moves mountains. Ace, if someone said to you: 'You can have everything you want!' what would your reaction be?"

When he continued without waiting for an answer, I silently thought: "Here we go again..."

"Surely you wouldn't accept his statement without thinking that he doesn't know what he's talking about, or yes, it may be possible, if only you had the money. Or, he's crazy! You may come up with many more negative reasons why you cannot have everything you want. The only time you would truly believe the statement is when the person is a multimillionaire and hands you a signed piece of paper, saying: 'This is my whole fortune – now it's yours!' Most of you don't know somebody that rich and generous. What a pity, for it means you don't know yourself.

"You do not realize your unlimited potential, Ace. All of you have self-imposed limitations, telling you or making you believe that 'I know I can't have everything I want'. If you blindly accept the statement without proof, you're a fool. On the other hand, you'll be an equal fool if you merely reject the statement as nonsense. Let me repeat: 'You can have everything you want!' Now what do you say?"

"How can you possibly..."

"Eheh, eheh," he interrupted bluntly. "That's one of your biggest problems – you've forgotten to ask 'How?' or 'Why?' As children you all did that but you were told: *'For ours is not to know'*, but to 'believe' or to 'have faith'. You were taught many truths like *'cast thy bread on the water...', 'seek and ye shall find...', 'knock, and for you shall be opened...'*

But when you asked: 'How?' or 'What does it mean?' or 'Why?'you always got the same answer:

'Just believe my child, and have faith...'

"Eheh, the answers you got from parents, teachers, clergymen, parsons and ministers were mostly the same: 'Just believe'. For those who attended Sunday school, the answers you got from well meaning but ignorant 18 year-old teachers were even worse, telling you that your sixpence worth of almonds would be taken to heaven by the angels, that same night, and given to Jesus who would then hand it to the poor. So you believed that and similar nonsense until one day you were rudely confronted with reality. No wonder most of you stopped asking questions, because you never got sensible answers."

Feeling guilty and deeply hurt I said: "Teecha, you obviously know I was such a person – like others I only tried my best."

"No offence, Ace – you were all in the same boat and got the same answers. Your mentors may have been 'the salt of the earth', but did they really make life a bit tastier? Eheh, some of the things you were told are indeed the basic truths of life and happiness, but still you don't seem to know how or why it works."

It didn't take me too long to ask: "OK Teecha, then what does it mean to 'have faith?'

"To be good at what you do or to be knowledgeable in any subject means that you understand the basics. We've analyzed existence and what a spirit is. We've explored the brain. We've defined the mind as the interaction between a spirit, its own body and brain, its environment and all other spirits. We've identified such entities as the creative or conscious mind and the subjective mind. Scar-face and his herd showed you what collective consciousness means and we've discussed the collective subconscious. Quite a mouthful. OK, Ace, so before I tell you what you can do with this power, some basics.

"Physically there is little difference between man and his closely related animal friends. His physical needs are similar, as are his safety and

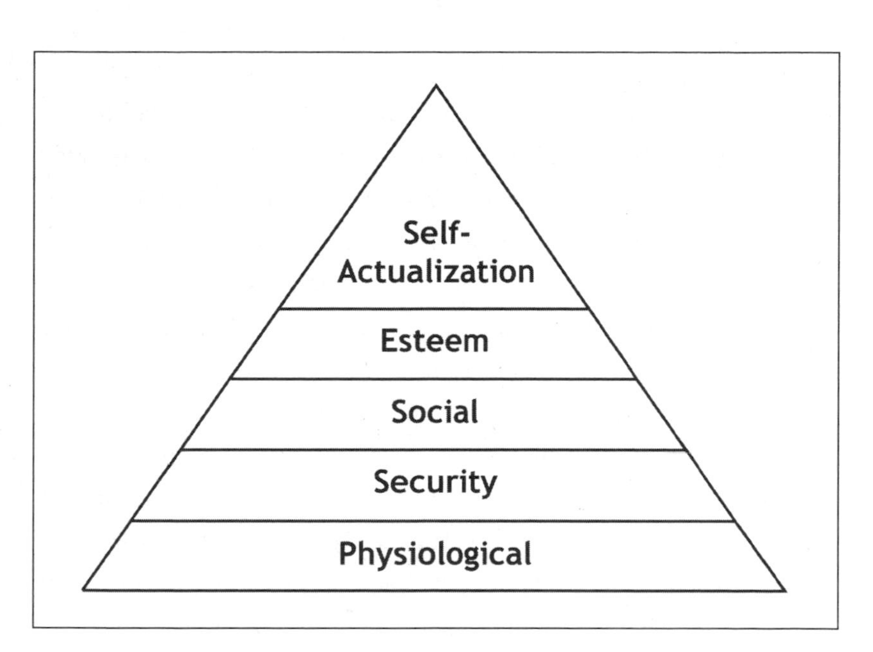

Fig 2: Basic Hierarchy of Needs

social needs. These basic needs of man and animals alike, have been categorized into a framework which explains the hierarchy into which these needs arrange themselves. It is usually depicted as a pyramid."

Teecha took his time and scratched another diagram on the sand, as shown in figure 2, then explained:

"The pyramid shows that certain needs have priority over others. Basic needs like food, clothing and shelter come first. Once these are satisfied, safety or security needs become dominant. At this second level a need exists to be free from physical danger and deprivation of the basics. Concern for the future becomes apparent, to ensure that physiological needs will be met. Once a reasonable level of security is reached, social or affiliation needs emerge. Since man and most other life forms are social spirits, you have a need to belong to and to be accepted by other beings of your own kind. You also have the need to be accepted by spirits on higher and lower levels than yourselves. Many animals affiliate themselves with humans, and most humans like to keep a pet or two.

“However, once a spirit belongs to a group of its own kind and level, the need for esteem arises. Feelings such as self-esteem, recognition, respect, social status, self-confidence, prestige and controlling others have to be experienced. If this is not properly satisfied, a spirit may go to extremes to get attention, often in a negative way by being disruptive or throwing a tantrum, like most politicians and extremists. At this stage any spirit has a difficult time coming to grips with his own spiritual existence.

“Once a spirit gets through this phase – and here we can draw the line between humans and most animals – maximizing one’s potential becomes important. As Abraham Maslow expressed it: ‘What a man can be, he must be.’ This desire to achieve or to become what a spirit is capable of, may be expressed in many ways. Fortunately you do not all have the same desires – that would have been utter chaos. At this stage, the top of the pyramid is reached. Accordingly, many of those who get there think they have ‘arrived’. Actually, Ace, this phase or achievement is just the beginning...”

“I certainly hope so Teecha, for I’m still no closer to understanding faith.” “Maybe you are but impatience won’t get you nearer. You’ll have to reconsider a few things, like this:

> *‘Teacher, which is the greatest commandment in the Law?’ Jesus replied:*
> *‘Love the Lord your God with all your* ***soul*** *and with all your* ***mind****.’ This is the first and greatest commandment. And the second is: ‘Love your neighbor as yourself.’*
> *‘All the Law and the Prophets hang on these two commandments.’*
> from Matthew 22 verses 36 to 40.

As he quoted the script with particular emphasis on certain words, I immediately knew that something was written between those lines which I had never understood and still didn’t understand. I queried: “Teecha, I know those words by heart but fail to see any connection with faith – they merely tell us to love God and one another... So?"

"*Tchi... tchi...* I'll have to tell you about recent discoveries in psychology and a few other things – maybe then you'll discover the real meaning behind those words. Having identified the conscious and subconscious minds, you all have led your psychologists to the basics of your make-up:

"Your conscious or creative mind, which is the *'I'* or spirit, acts or reacts only on information that it receives through all your senses, and you may as well accept that there are many more than five. This information could also come from a spirit's own conscious will or imagination, in other words from within itself. It correlates this information almost instantly with its memory banks and decides on an appropriate action for every situation.

"One of these senses or sources of information is the subjective mind. If you think back to your Pheon, this subjective mind relies on information from the subconscious mind, the creative subconscious mind, the collective conscious and collective subconscious minds and the Universal Mind. It is important Ace, to realize that the subjective mind also relies on information from the creative or conscious mind. Thus, one mind relies on the other, which relies on the other. All your minds are totally interdependent."

We were sitting underneath the shade of the big umbrella thorn. Teecha got up and went to fetch his digging stick. As he walked away, I once more wondered about him. The things he showed me and told me about the bush were the things of a Bushman. But whoever else he was, the old man had become more to me than a friend – he had crept into my heart. My body jerked as my mind battled with painful thoughts: I had to return home, and after that I'd probably never see him again. I wanted to stay with him, like a little boy with his father, or to come back some day and to find him again, but knew it wasn't meant to be.

Returning to the shade he handed me the canvas water bag and then drew a number of circles on the sand. Even Xi'tau, lying in his favorite

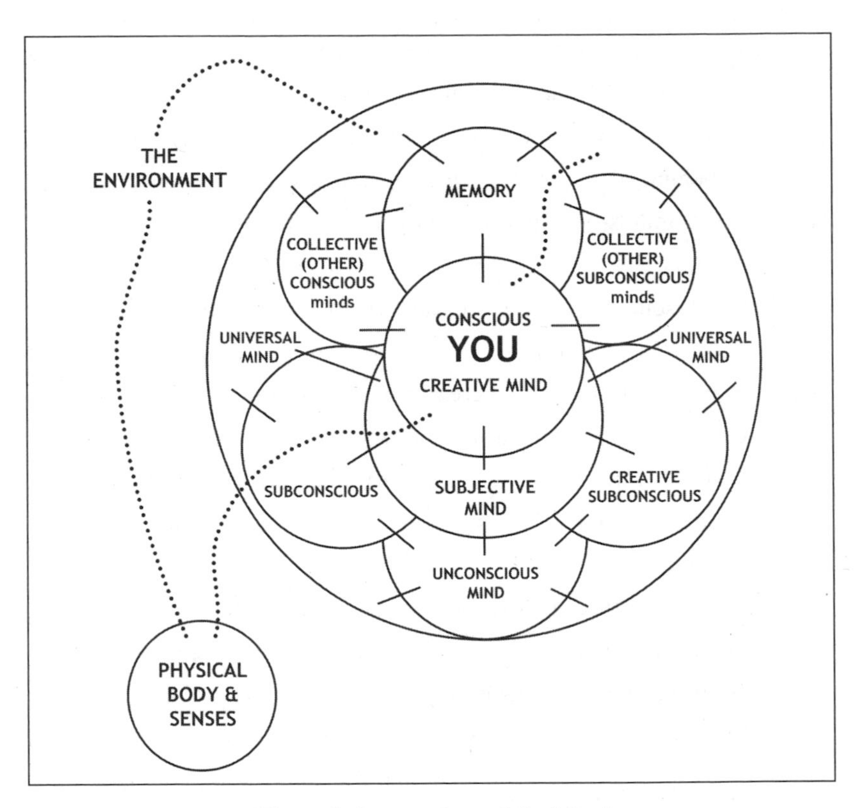

Figure 3: Interactions of the Mind

position on his back with his paws in the air, flopped round and watched with some interest. Taking a sip of cool water I realized how little there must be left.

"Teecha, I'll have to leave tomorrow."

A scratching stick was the comment received. His diagram is shown in figure 3.

When he had finished drawing it, I forgot about leaving.

"From this diagram of interconnecting circles you can see how a spirit receives 'input' from his various minds and how he influences all those minds with his own 'output'."

He hesitated slightly and continued with a giggle:

"Bear in mind, Ace, that a spirit has to take its memory into account, which plays a major role in the whole act. In fact, memory is often the director of all the action.

"Apart from this, a spirit has to collate all the input from its bodily senses too – sight, sound, taste, touch and smell, all the time. What a job. Indeed, any spirit is a very clever entity.

"Of importance is that the subjective mind cannot distinguish nor identify its source of information – because it doesn't have to. The sole purpose of the subjective mind is to analyze information and to suggest appropriate actions to the spirit, which of course, the spirit can either accept or reject. You sometimes say: 'I knew I shouldn't have done that', or 'I'm doing this against my better judgment'. One of your problems is that your subjective mind is often wrong, but fortunately your conscious mind has the final say."

"Why would our subjective minds be wrong? "I'll tell you, but right now you should be able to realize why 'All the Law and the Prophets' hang on two commandments." "Sorry Teecha, I still don't."

"Ace, there is another balance: between any one individual *'I'* and all other beings. No *'I'* can exist independently from others because it is a part of the Whole or Ultimate Spirit or God. We are obliged to love the Ultimate Spirit because we're one with it, and we are obliged to love all other spirits, human or not, because we're one with them too. Remember that the subjective mind cannot tell where it gets its input from – it merely receives, analyzes and stores information for the conscious mind to use, as and when required. This is of the utmost importance. For example, when you say 'You stupid fool!' to someone or whether you say it to yourself, it is all the same to the subjective mind. It only records the information 'You stupid fool', and stores that for future use by the conscious mind.

"At a later stage, when this information is retrieved, the word 'You' means somebody else or you yourself, and the conscious mind accepts either or both meanings. When the subjective supplies data to the *'I'*, it makes no distinction as to whom the word 'You' refers, leaving the conscious mind to 'make up its mind'. Thus, the more negative thoughts you have about others, the more problems you have with yourself as you are in fact, telling yourself 'Stupid fool' all the time.

"Although your subjective mind is exceptionally clever, it has no power of differentiation. Unlike the conscious, it cannot distinguish between you and me and somebody else! It accepts something like 'love' as an entity in itself, no matter from where it originates and it does so with all your emotions. This is the first basic and important fact about the subjective mind.

"You worried about your water situation a few minutes ago only because I gave you some to drink. The mind generally functions by means of a process called 'association'. It associates different events and happenings with similar incidents from its memory banks. Whenever a few friends have a good time telling jokes, one joke often leads to another because the mind very quickly finds something in one joke that triggers off another. Our 'stupid fool' example works in exactly the same way. The next time a spirit consciously requests information relating to a similar situation, or subconsciously the subjective associates a situation to similar events, part of all the instantaneously retrieved information will contain 'You stupid fool' and the conscious mind takes action, accordingly.

"Imagine, Ace, what could happen if that was an all important bit of information which a spirit needed to make a decision about its own abilities? How often do you, verbally or mentally, convey that 'stupid fool' concept in your everyday life?"

A piece of the puzzle fell into place and the picture took on a new dimension. Teecha knew that. "Eheh, Ace, now you realize the importance of those two commandments: If you do not love your neighbor, you cannot love yourself, and if you don't love yourself, you cannot love anything else!

"You could replace the word 'love' with many others, like respect, pardon, enjoy or uplift. We are back to the balance of everything once more. If you think something of yourself, you cannot do otherwise but think something of others. When you think nothing of others, you think exactly the same of yourself."

I must have looked too serious for he continued dryly: "You can, of course, go totally overboard, thinking so much of yourself that nobody else needs to think something of you."

It worked and I had to smile, but there were many other things on my mind: a long, hot and lonely drive to the border not knowing where I'd find water, no air-conditioning and hopefully enough fuel. I had lost track of what day it was and wondered if my story would hold water back home.

Teecha interrupted my thoughts: "Ace, stop worrying about water because we'll make a plan – you're the one who needs to know what faith really means."

"Time is my problem, Teecha. I'd like to know more but..."

"*Tchi... tchi...* There is eternity you know – another day or two will make no difference, except to you."

He continued as if I had no other option but to stay:

"Apart from the trouble it has with differentiation, your subjective mind is extremely clever. It constantly receives information from all the senses and simultaneously filters and sorts it all out. Rather than clutter the conscious mind with useless information, the subjective mind analyzes and controls what the conscious mind needs to know or wants to know. I'll use an example to make this clear, as it is the second basic but important fact about your subjective mind:

"When you were learning to ride a bicycle or to drive a car, your conscious mind struggled to do what was necessary to balance yourself on top of the bicycle, to pedal and steer it, and what to do when you wanted to stop – you came up short quite a few times, didn't you Ace? However, when the knowledge is gained, the conscious mind simply lets the subjective take control and doesn't have a thing to worry about. Once you're able to ride a bicycle there is little left for the conscious mind to do. Years after learning to ride that bicycle your subconscious still handles it and will only alert the conscious mind if it cannot make its own decision.

"Consider what happens when you get the idea to buy a new car. As soon as you decide on maybe two or three types of cars as a possible choice, you start seeing many of those particular cars all around you, and more so once you've 'made up your mind'. It is not that there are suddenly more of those cars around today than there were yesterday, it is just because you now want to be aware of them so you see them. Ace, your subjective mind acts on and controls what the conscious mind needs to or wants to know. The spiritual desire of wanting to know is a force to reckon with.

"There is a third basic but important fact about your subjective mind, so I'll tell you a short story:

Bulahr and his wife had been living in the cold forests of Tajen for many years. Their life was happy and simple – they lived off the land and especially during the warmer sun periods, the forests provided them with an abundance of food. During the cold periods food became scarce, but Bulahr was a shrewd hunter and they always had enough to eat. Less than one sun period ago Faliha, his wife, had a baby daughter and very soon she became a joy in their lives.

They also had a female wolf as a pet. Bulahr found her as a pup, injured, abandoned and hungry in a ravine, more than four sun periods ago. Faliha nursed the little wolf until she was well, hoping that she would return to the forest sometime. Instead, she decided to stay and they named her Ta-cha, meaning 'from the snow'.

As Bulahr was cautiously stalking a young deer his mind was elsewhere: how things had changed since the last four moons. Why did his lovely Faliha pick such a bad time to die? How was it possible that she had fallen down those cliffs? She knew them so well, always pleasing him with a handful of tasty *thoht* berries, which were only found on the mountain Gemynd, not too far from their cabin.

The terrible sadness of her untimely death almost overcame him, but quickly he took control of himself, just when the deer started to sense danger. Bulahr was lucky; his arrow struck it right in the heart, killing it instantly. He felt sorry for the animal as he had never liked killing any of the animals in the forest, but at least now they would have food for a few days. He thought about the fact that he had left Faliha lying in the snow, according to their custom, and how the wild wolves had ripped her body apart. Swiftly he slit the deer's throat, then hastily slung it over his shoulders and started back. It was getting late and the smell of blood would attract the wolves. He knew they were around, and to encounter them now would mean he would have to leave the deer for them, in order to save his own life. As he hurried back through the deep snow his mind wandered again:

If only this cold period would come to an end so that he could get to the village for help. He found it difficult to cope with little Whaliti who needed constant attention and food. Every so often he had to go out hunting and looking for food, leaving the baby behind. How fortunate Ta-cha was there to guard the baby when he was out. He often wondered why she was not like the other wolves, having none of their vicious character. This afternoon, he had put Whaliti to sleep in her cot, covered her with warm skins and left for the hunt. He knew she would be safe because Ta-cha just curled up on the floor next to the cot, knowing that he wanted her to stay. She'll be hungry too, and would appreciate some of the deer.

As he approached the log cabin he started to feel uneasy, and as he dropped the deer by the door, he sensed that something was terribly wrong. Ta-cha didn't come to greet him. Gripping his axe he moved slowly through the door. Ta-cha got up from the corner and limped towards him, softly whining, head down. She was covered in blood, some still dripping from her jaws. Bulahr glanced at the cot – the baby was gone. Blood stains everywhere. In a flash his mind said: 'Once a wolf, always a wolf...' Blinded by anger, frustration and hate, he swung his axe high in the air and brought it down crashing through Ta-cha's skull, again, and again. Eventually his rage subsided and he fell sobbing onto his knees, his spirit broken. He should have known this could happen – what a fool he was.

A faint whimper came from somewhere. He jumped up again. It sounded like Whaliti. How was it possible? Where is she? His eyes flying round the cabin, a new scene met him. Inside lay two other dead wolves – and there a third, almost dead, with its throat ripped open. Was that what he had heard? No, there was the whimper again, from underneath the cot. Rushing forward, he clawed at the bundle of skins and hides lying there: Inside was his daughter, safely hidden away and unharmed...

Teecha stopped talking. I got up, walked a few meters and noticed that the mirages on the horizon blurred more than usual – dust in the air or something. Without looking at him, I said: "No, it can't be... The idiot. Shit, Teecha, that's a rotten story."

"Eheh, and now you have all sorts of mixed feelings. Why, Ace? It didn't happen to you... or did it? Were you there, did you actually see it? No, only because I've tricked you into letting your imagination run loose are you experiencing these emotions. You saw or imagined the scenes in your mind only, with startling results. This explains the third and most important fact about your subjective mind: It cannot distinguish between reality and imagination – it receives, analyzes and stores information, and that's all it does.

"The incredible power of imagination lies within the conscious mind only. It can imagine something so vividly that the subjective mind receives it as factual and acts accordingly, by receiving the imaginary impulses as truth, analyzing them and then supplying the conscious mind with possible actions, to the extent of suggesting what emotions 'should' be experienced. The story also shows you what collective consciousness means, by you having empathy with all the actors that you've never met, including and probably more for Ta-cha the wolf.

"Take this thing called imagination a little further. Consider that every idea we have or any action we take, starts off in the labyrinths of imagination in the conscious mind. This is quite true; when you get the idea to have a cup of tea or coffee, you're just imagining the fact that you're drinking a cup of whatever in the near future – you're not drinking it now, unless you had the same idea a while back. Likewise, if you get the idea to buy a new car you're imagining yourself behind the steering wheel, driving it, smelling the new leather seats, hearing its engine and feeling its power. Here's something else to test your imagine-power with..."

"Hey, no more of that – I don't like sad stories."

"There is this juicy and appetizing looking yellow fruit, 'and the lemon's flower is sweet'... Now take a good bite out of it..."

My mouth watered and I swallowed.

"What's that in your mouth, Ace? A real piece of lemon?"

I swallowed again.

"Now you know what imagination can do and how your subjective mind reacts to it, unable to distinguish it from reality."

"OK, Teecha, I get the point, now what are you trying to tell me?"

"A minute or so ago we came up with the idea or thought to drink a cup of tea. Using that as an analogy will explain what faith is all about: You have set a simple goal – to drink a cup of tea. You imagine the fact that you are drinking that cup of tea. However, it will not become reality unless you do something about it.

"So, you have a number of options: You either ask somebody to make it for you, you go to a cafe and buy a cup of tea or you make it yourself. You decide on the last option, which means you have to take many actions, more or less in some sequence, before you will actually drink it.

"One of Murphy's laws states: 'Whatever you want to do, you have to do something else first'. So you get up, go to the kitchen, pour water into the kettle, boil the water, find the tea, put some in the teapot, pour boiling water over it, let it brew, find the milk and sugar, pour the tea in a cup, find a teaspoon, stir the tea and finally you sit down and drink it... By the way, it sounds like a good idea right now, don't you think?"

"Wily old man!" I thought. "OK, I'll make us some."

While I made tea he continued: "What a process, Ace – assuming you don't encounter any hassles. In everyday life you may have to overcome a number of obstacles before you can drink your tea. How about this: the kettle burnt out, there was no water in the tap, the electricity supply was cut, you forgot to buy tea, you dropped the cup of tea on the floor – 'many a slip between cup and lip' – or you realized too late that the milk was sour. Would you allow any of those to stop you from having your tea? No, even if you can't have it now but a little later, you will calmly or otherwise, set about overcoming any obstacle preventing you from having your cup of tea. You could make a fire to boil the water, you could use a pan to substitute the burnt out kettle, you could borrow tea from your neighbor, find another cup or pick up the pieces of the shattered cup and glue them together again, if it was your only cup. Nothing could really stop you from drinking that cup of tea... Or would you give up halfway Ace, telling yourself it was 'sour grapes'?"

I didn't encounter any hassles – there was hot water in the thermos flask and two tea bags later I handed him his. As usual, he took the mug with both hands and held it without using its handle and continued:

"What it all boils down to Ace, is that you set your mind on having a cup of tea, all starting from imagination. No little problem is going to deprive you of it and you may have to resort to all sorts of ingenious ways to eventuality drink it. You know that if you want or need a cup of tea you can have it. If you apply this simple example to any other idea or any other thing you can imagine, what's the difference? Whether it's buying that fancy car, going overseas, starting your own business or realizing your life long ambition, it's all the same. Achieving your goal may take a little longer than making a cup of tea, it may require a bit more effort and you may encounter more hassles, but that is the only difference – you can have your slice of the cake, any size, and eat it..."

He had this clever way of hinting, so I put my cup down, walked over to the vehicle and fetched a cookie jar from the food trunk. Hopefully Xi'tau had missed spraying the food trunk, because everything else smelt of lion's spray. Offering him some biscuits I asked: "Is it really that simple, Teecha?"

"Thank you. Eheh, the only prerequisite is that you must know, not wish, what you want in life. This may sound too simple as well, but few people really know what they want, let alone have any plans for achieving their goals. Surveys have shown that as little as two people in a thousand have some idea of what they want from life.

"Knowledge of how and why the powers of the mind work is a bonus. Without knowledge of what you want, what is important to you and what will make you happy, nothing else could help you. Not luck, not intelligence, not health, not degrees, not a strong personality, nothing. Not even a windfall of millions of dollars. If you don't know what you want in life, riches become a misery. Once you know what you want, and know that it is possible to get it, once you know who and what you are, and know that the balance is eternal and you know where you're going, only then can you use a few more tricks to help you along.

"These tricks make you lucky, clever, healthy, and give you a radiant personality, as you're starting to use your real potential.

"I'll teach you one trick which may have a dramatic influence on your life, but instead of upsetting your emotions like life's little stories do, it allows you to control them. It allows you to control almost anything in your life, including your future."

"Control my own future?"

"Eheh. It takes a bit of practise, though, about 15 minutes at a time, but it is extremely powerful. In fact, you should use it with caution, as it may well be too powerful. But there is nothing much to this trick, except believing or knowing that it works."

I shook my head in disbelief and Teecha said: "Ace, haven't we gone through enough aspects of a spirit and its minds for you to accept that after all, it may just be possible to flip a tennis ball inside out? If you're still skeptical about your powers then forget about it."

"No, wait... I know I must learn and accept many more things, but it is difficult to change old beliefs – I don't know why. Please tell me how it works."

Teecha looked at me for a long time, as if trying to decide whether it was worth the effort sharing any of life's secrets with me. Just when I thought that he had made up his mind not to, he murmured to himself: "This one insists on being difficult."

Another minute or so passed before he responded again:

"You all have many everyday decisions, Ace, you all have worries and uncertainties. You may be worried about clinching that sale tomorrow, how your presentation to the board of directors will go, or whether the bank manager will grant you that all-important loan. You may be concerned about the decision to take up a new job or to start your own business. You may want to reach somebody else where words have failed. To use this trick you must know exactly what you want to achieve and how you are going to do it. For example, you want and need a loan from the bank to reach your goal. Secondly, you must find a place where you will not be disturbed at all for ten minutes where you can make yourself as comfortable as possible: maybe the study, the bedroom or in a park or a quiet spot in the countryside. There should be as little noise possible to distract you. Thirdly you must be totally alert, not tired and most definitely not drugged in any way. Now make yourself comfortable and close your eyes...

"Before you do anything else you must be completely relaxed, both in mind and body. Think every muscle into complete relaxation. It is achieved step by step from each toe to the legs, each finger to the arms, then your stomach, back and neck. Once you know you are completely relaxed, take a few slow deep breaths and relax even more. All the time, though, stay alert and do not fall asleep – you are not trying self-hypnosis and you are not going to meditate. Then start to count from 1 to 20, slowly, and take a few long breaths between each count.

"With every count, think that you are putting your mind into a higher state of awareness, directed all the time at what you initially wanted to do or know. Get your mind completely focused on that one thing of importance. While counting, get rid of all other influences, thoughts or distractions. Forget about everything else and change your mind into the highest gear possible.

"Once you get to the count of 20, you should end up in a very high state of awareness and consciousness, but far removed from a trance. Some of your psychological experts call this the 'alpha' state of mind. They're quite right, as this is the first state of mind, like when you were a child and your mind was actively relaxed, open, questing, responsive, demanding, learning, receptive, controlling, and vivid with imagination. Anyway, all the time, you must concentrate on what you want to do or what you want to know! Now wave the magic wand...

******

"If it was the bank manager you're after, see yourself explaining your reasons, look him in the eyes and answer his questions. Convince him of your reasons for wanting the loan and watch his reactions. It is quite possible that you may reach him telepathically at this stage, so ensure that you have a good case beforehand. Finally, sign the piece of paper that he puts under your nose and make sure to thank him, exactly as it will be tomorrow or whenever you have your meeting.

"You may do the same with the MD of the company that has to sign your contract tomorrow, or you may discuss the whole issue of starting your own business with your would-be clients and what service they're going to expect from you. Imagine the whole scene, exactly as it will be. Talk to the person you want to reach, listen to his or her problems and why he or she doesn't want to or can't communicate with you – discuss it all. You'll be surprised, if your case is well prepared, to see the results of your future achievement – it is all happening your way.

"It has already happened. If it is that all-important speech you 'delivered' tomorrow, or that final match that you 'won' next Saturday – the audience is giving you a standing ovation. "Then ever so slowly, ease yourself from imagination to reality. Start counting back from 20 to 1 to allow your mind to take over its normal functions of keeping you in the present. Open your eyes and you will know that you have already achieved what you had set out to do, or that you have the answers to your questions."

******

"It sounds fascinating, Teecha, but you say it's not hypnosis or meditation. Why does it work? Is it something to do with faith?"

"Another drawback the subjective mind has, apart from not being able to distinguish between reality and imagination, is that it doesn't know the difference between past, present and future. This is a powerful tool for the conscious mind if you know how to control it, but extremely detrimental otherwise. You can do anything with this little trick but hopefully you'll only use it to the benefit of all concerned. To try and use it for any other purpose will be to your own loss. Eheh, Ace, it is based on the true power of faith. To emphasize that power, I'll give you a few examples where the same principles are used negatively. These examples are dangerous and destructive if practiced, but show exactly what faith means:

"A few people could conspire to tell their victim as soon as they meet him individually for the first time on a particular day, that he looks pale and ill and to ask him what is wrong. They would say things like: 'My, you look awful'or 'Is anything the matter? Why don't you lie down?' or 'You should be in bed'. It takes a very strong personality not to fall for the negative power of faith. In most cases the unfortunate subject quickly develops some or other psychosomatic illness, enough to really put him in bed for a few days or even in hospital.

"Casting a spell on somebody is very real. You will know Ace, that in Africa many indigenous tribes believe sincerely in the powers of the *sangoma* or the witchdoctor. If someone has a grudge against his neighbor and if he is able to pay the *sangoma* enough, the witchdoctor may cast a spell over the unfortunate rival or his whole family. The witchdoctor may also send the '*Tokoloshe*' to such a person's home. The *Tokoloshe* is a person that was brought up inside a large clay pot since childhood, bow-legged and hunchbacked, living at the mercy of the witchdoctor who would use him on occasion to poison food or to murder somebody.

"Some people fear the Tokoloshe to such an extent that they put bricks under their beds to lift them higher from the ground, as the Tokoloshe is obviously short and crippled, having been brought up in a clay pot. The casting of the spell or the fact that the Tokoloshe had been to somebody's home is made known to the community. Because of a deep collective belief or faith in the witchdoctor's powers, disaster and bad luck soon strike the unfortunate person, to the extent of disease infecting livestock or his family dying from unknown illnesses to lightning setting his home on fire.

"Your Western religions and teachings will be quick to laugh off and discard these beliefs as superstitious rubbish, thereby missing the point of what they try to preach themselves: Sincere faith is an awesome power – positively or negatively.

"Knowing what you need and want, believing in yourself and others, and having faith in the fact that you can have everything, are the basics of a great and universal power. If faith is so powerful when used negatively or believing in negative and evil things, then it is certainly as powerful when used positively. The choice is yours, but be warned: it's not intended for acquiring wealth – that's a by-product. You could use this power to obtain that, to roll around in a room full of money, but you'll soon find that you've tricked yourself, if that was your only 'want'.

"Otherwise, once you know your real needs it's simple. Don't be scared to use the Power. Prominent people in all spheres of life do exactly that. Tennis players, formula one racing drivers, successful business executives and politicians use this same method to reach the top in their field and to stay on top.

"It is more than positive thinking, although that is as important for your attitude to life. Faith is a case of controlling the future, by letting your subjective mind understand what you really want or need (like the cup of tea) and then putting it to work.

"Applying true faith is called by many names: auto-suggestion, psycho-cybernectics, self-imaginary, dynamic psychology, mind-dynamics and others. It was supposedly discovered during the 1940s and early 1950s, when it was found that most successful people used their imagination more effectively than others, and also knew what they wanted. But yet again, Ace, it is not something that you invented nor discovered in this age.

"The *Brihadaranyaka Upanishad* states clearly:

'As a man acts, so does he become,
As a man's desire is, so is his destiny.'"

****

THE SEVENTH DAY

For some reason or other I had no appetite the previous evening. Teecha fried another piece of puff adder in the coals and enjoyed his meal. He salted what was left of the snake and hung it over the branches of a hook thorn tree. Nothing much apart from insects would have been able to get past those thorns, so his larder was safe. Still smacking his lips he took a spade and walked into the open, where he started to dig a hole in the sand about six feet or two meters in diameter, slanting to half a meter deep.

Watching him curiously, I tried to whittle a spoon from a piece of russet bush-willow wood. Not having the slightest idea of what he was up to I waited for him to explain something about his laborious effort. He didn't. Adding the finishing touches to his miniature crater, he asked me if I had a waterproof ground-sheet.

"What for?"

"To catch the rain."

"Rain? Oh yes – next summer." I thought he'd like to have a sail like that for future use and immediately decided to give him one, as there were two or three in the back of the vehicle.

"Just a minute." I walked to the vehicle and abruptly stopped ten feet or three meters away from it – Xi'tau was lying on his roof carrier bed. He lifted his big head and stared at me for a second or two. As if I was nothing to be concerned about, he yawned loudly and continued his nap.

"Now don't be silly," I said to myself, "that cat saved your life."

I promptly continued to the back of the vehicle and scratched around for one of the ground-sheets. Xi'tau thought little of my disturbance – in fact, he was snoring all the way to dreamland.

Handing the ground-sheet to Teecha I said: "It's yours – keep it."

"No, Ace, I have no use for it, but you'll need water on your way back and it will rain tomorrow."

I was immediately reminded that I had to get back to the big city and my mood changed drastically. By now I was days late and without doubt, my family would have listed me as a missing person. Thinking about my irresponsibility and what I was going to tell them, I noticed that Teecha was laying the ground-sheet over the hole, throwing sand over the corners to keep it down.

"He must know that some nights it's possible to catch a liter of water or more that way from dew," I thought. For me it would have been barely enough to last one day in the heat, but I realized that every drop counts and recalled his promise to make a plan.

I was about to tell him that he had a clever idea, when I was suddenly struck by what he had said a few seconds earlier.

"You think it's going to rain?"

"Eheh, you may want to cover some of your things."

"Teecha, there's not a cloud in sight and it's past the rain-season. What on earth makes you think it will rain?"

"Termites."

"Termites? You mean ants? Come on, Teecha, you're having me on – are you serious?" "Eheh, they've been unusually active since the day before yesterday. This evening some eager ones already left their nests. They only fly when it's going to rain – and soon."

Having learned to respect his judgment, or maybe just to make him feel good, I half-heartedly packed some stuff away and covered the chairs and a few other articles with the remaining ground-sheets. I was about to say goodnight when I noticed that Teecha was already fast asleep close to the fire. For a while I stared at the old man, wondering. It was chilly and I poured myself a nightcap. As I turned in, Xi'tau started roaring from the top of his bed, a mere ten meters from my tent. If ever I realized why a lion's roar could be heard kilometers away it was that night: the ground and the air literally trembled. So did I.

From a deep state of mental and physical inactivity I woke with a jerk and sat up straight.

"What the heck was that?"

The next instant the tent lit up inside and a few seconds later the air trembled again – this time from a loud thunder clap. I couldn't believe my eyes and ears. Lying down again, I waited for the next lightning flash and mumbled:

"Typical of the Kalahari – totally unpredictable."

Then I recalled Teecha's interest in the ants over the last two days and wondered if it really was so unpredictable. Sure enough, another bright flash, followed by a deafening crack and then rumbling noise into the distance.

Thunder showers rather than continuous rain, make up for the greater percentage of rainfall in southern Africa. Knowing their pattern quite well, I said to myself: "Here we go again..." and waited.

Within ten minutes we were in the midst of an electric storm. Strong winds lashed and ripped at the tent, lightning flashed and thunderbolts cracked continuously. Outside chairs and tables were blown over by the wind, sending pots and pans smashing to the ground.

No rain yet, but I knew it wouldn't take long. The first big drops splattered onto the tent. Crawling out, I coughed and choked from dust and had to shield my eyes from flying sand. There was a strong smell of sulphur in the air.

"Teecha!" I shouted, but my voice had no effect in the storm. In the psychedelic lightning flashes, I saw him checking his waterhole.

"Teecha! Come..." I shouted again and beckoned as I ran towards him. Lightning kills many people in Africa. One of the safest places to be during a thunderstorm is inside any vehicle, the metal frame around you acting as a 'Faraday cage'. Gripping Teecha by his arm and push-pulling him away from the hole towards the 4x4, I felt I was being in control of myself for the first time in many days as I commanded: "Forget it – come with me!"

Before we could reach the vehicle, the rain came pouring down. I jumped into the front seat and opened the door on the other side. Teecha ran around and jumped in too. By then we were both wet through and cold to the bone. Outside, blue-white sheets of water thrashed around in the whirling wind, like blowing silk curtains seen through intermittent light.

For the second time that night I stared at the Bushman. Every now and then his dark silhouette brightened from the lightning, but his face remained expressionless as he watched the rain. I wondered some more.

"Where is Xi'tau?" I asked after a long silence, surprised at my sudden concern for the lion.

"Underneath your vehicle – don't worry Ace, he'll be fine."

The impossibility of the situation dawned on me and I had to smile. There I was, truly in the middle of nowhere, inside my 4x4 thrashed at by a heavy storm, a strange wet Bushman next to me and a gigantic lion sheltering underneath it.

"What next?" I mumbled. Looking around for a cigarette I remembered that my last packet was in the tent.

"You smoke too much," Teecha warned, and then remarked as if everything was completely normal: "The ants are always right".

The storm ended as suddenly as it started. After some alarmingly close lightning bolts and squalls of wind between the pelting rain, it was all over. The storm had lasted less than an hour and a dim glow in the East announced a new day. Stepping out I promptly shone a torch underneath the vehicle, still concerned about Xi'tau. If he had been human, I would have gazed at a miserable, wet and dismayed face – the lion was obviously not happy with his circumstances. I started to grin but then tactfully (it seems to be the right word) left him to his misery and summed up the situation in camp. Everything was wet. More than that, everything was soaked and scattered all over the place. It was cold and unlike the past few mornings, there were no hot coals to restart the fire. No dry wood either.

I unpacked a gas-cooker and blew as much water as was possible away from the element. I did the same with a wet cigarette lighter and eventually a 'flick of the Bic' did the trick. I remembered Teecha's waterhole. Apart from a layer of sand and dust at the bottom, it contained at least three inches of crystal clear water, more than enough to last me on my trip back. I cupped my hand and tasted it – ice cold and refreshing. I was on my knees filling a jug to fill the kettle, when Teecha said from behind: “That should do you fine, Ace.”

Sipping hot coffee, I became aware of the beauty around me. The thunderstorm had found something else do, as bright sun-rays shone through menacing but retreating black clouds, turning the sky into a kaleidoscope. Droplets of water on the grass, shrubs and trees reflected pure gold. A rainbow boasted its colorful arc across the sky. As Teecha and I watched it, a remarkable sight happened before our eyes. There was half a moon in the sky, almost directly above, which competed with its own pure white rainbow against that of the rising sun. Two arches of light appeared in the sky, one crossing the other. Never before and never since have I seen anything like it. At some stage, for a few seconds, that brilliant white yet almost colorless moon rainbow outshone the beauty of the sun’s possessive play with light. If ever I had the opportunity to say that something was ‘too beautiful for words’, that was it, but by the time I thought about the camera, it was too late.

“N!odima gave us a good sign Ace – few people ever see this. I saw a moonbow once before, but not crossed with that of the sun. A long time ago my great grandmother tried to describe to me that she had seen something similar. What she told me at the time I had laughed off as an old woman’s fancy. Today I’ll pray for her forgiveness, as words could never give justice to what you and I were fortunate to experience. She said that what she saw was the sign of Love.”

There was a long silence as we both kept looking at the sky, as if by doing that might bring the spectacle back. After a while, I decided that Teecha was getting too occupied with the clouds or his memories and touched his shoulder, just to ensure that he was still with me. He responded with a jerk that frightened us both but then he calmly and matter-of-factly said: “It was Pula. Pula was there with a friend. Pula is no longer with us, but her friend is – she’s watching over you. I’ll see you now-now.”

He jogged away into the bush. The word ‘pula’ means rain in

Se'Tswana, and I couldn't figure what Teecha meant by the rain subsiding while 'her friend' was watching me. Xi'tau crawled out from underneath the 4x4, stretched and smelled the air. After a while he scratched a hollow in the wet sand and promptly lay down in it. Turning over onto his back, he wiggled and twitched from side to side. For the first time during the last few days I was completely alone with the lion but I didn't even realize it. He just reminded me of my own sand bath. A minute or two later though he sniffed around and disappeared in Teecha's direction.

Somebody had to do something about the chaos, so I unpacked all the wet equipment, hung some things up to dry and put others out in the sun. After all the reorganizing and cleaning, I finally sat down on a wet chair. By then the sun was shining brightly. Sitting quietly on my own, I noticed the difference between that morning and those of the previous few days. It was as if there was a new life in everything around me. Birds chirpingly jumped and fluttered in the shrubs, insects buzzed around, and bright colored butterflies perched in colonies on the wet sand, sipping up the moisture with their long proboscus. Mice and little shrews ran through the grass and up and down tree trunks. As I watched their activities and those of the birds more closely, I realized they were all after a delicacy: flying ants.

After a good rain, hundreds of thousands of winged termites leave their nests, with one goal in life – to start a new colony. Only a few pairs of the strongest or luckiest will survive. After mating, the female becomes the ungainly fat queen of the new nest, unable to move at all. Her only purpose in life is to lay eggs – up to 36,000 each day. Such a nest or mound may survive for hundreds of years. Unfortunately for the flying ants but fortunately for many other life forms, there are few survivors. Their flimsy wings last for only a few hundred meters. After shedding them, there is frantic action on the ground as males chase after females, each male trying to outwit his peers in impressing a princess. However, their chances of surviving, mating and starting a new colony in the soft wet soil are slim, as they are preyed upon in the air and on the ground by just about every other living creature.

The activities of life and song were catchy though. Destructive as the storm may have been, it is the lifeblood of the Kalahari. I felt like joining the festivities.

"Actually, life is not a bitch – it's a miracle," I decided, and wished that I could share the experience of that day with my love.

I was still daydreaming when I heard Teecha coming back. A happy and strangely familiar tune from his pipe sounded closer and closer. He arrived dancing to his own music with half a dozen empty ostrich eggs in his skin bag. As he put them down next to the waterhole, he said smiling: "They need a refill."

He took a jug and scooping water, filled them all through the small hole in each shell. Then he sealed the holes carefully with grass and a mixture of beeswax and gum from sweet thorn trees.

"What are you going to do with them now?" I asked.

"Oh, bury them in the sand somewhere, for the times when I'll really need water."

I fetched a 20-liter water can from the vehicle and started filling it. Soon the can was full and I got another. The second one was more than half full before Teecha's rain catcher was empty.

The beauty of that day, pulsating with life, filled me with joy and a zest for living. It was difficult to imagine the existence of another real world: one full of misery, heartbreaks, toil and wars, one where the futile pursuit of pieces of green and pink paper was believed to be the prerequisite for happiness and peace. I knew that I had to go back to it and the mere thought changed my mood again, like the night before. I missed my kids and once more I wished that she was there too.

"Teecha, are you married?"

"Ke gona... but Pula left for the world of spirits a long time ago."

"I'm sorry to hear that," I condoled, but prodded further:

"Did you love her?"

"Eheh, Pula and I are one." Only then did I realize who Pula and her friend really was, so it took me a few moments to respond:

"She has a beautiful name... Do you still love her?"

"Eheh, why do you ask?"

"Why?"

"Why what?"

"Why do you still love her?

"That 'why' I honestly can't explain Ace. Why do you love your wife? Just like you do, she thinks and is concerned about you all the time. The two of you wasted a love that many people envied. However, you can still do something about it. Normally you receive a gift like yours only once, but you had two chances. Both of you should have been killed that night on the road if it wasn't for the white light that kept your vehicle on the road."

Shocked cold by his knowledge of my past, I tried to shout but my throat had turned dry:

"Who told you about my wife and how do you know about the light?"

He kept quiet, took out his pipe and started playing sadly.

"Dammit, Teecha," I swallowed twice and burst out again. "You know more about me than I do myself! Who the bloody hell are you?"

Still he didn't reply and kept on playing that sad melody. I felt like shaking him by the shoulders and was about to scream-demand an explanation when I noticed something. The pain and frustration of my own heart reflected back from the sudden and watery sadness of two empathic eyes. All I eventually managed was: "OK, I'm sorry – forget it."

A good minute or two later I tried to change the subject. "Teecha, why is it that sometimes we are so happy, like the birds today, and some days life is so difficult?"

He stopped playing and put the pipe bag into his bag, but didn't answer me, so I continued: "Wouldn't it be nice if we could always be happy?"

Still no reaction. Discouraged by then, I almost pleaded: "In fact Teecha, right now I don't even see a reason for life – what is the purpose of it and where does it lead to?"

After a long silence I was about to get up and start packing for my trip back when he finally spoke:

"Come my friend, let's walk and I'll tell you what I know..."

******

DESTINY

The ship of the mind set sail
to the place called Destiny;
All there is to her avail
– the Wisdom of Eternity...

"Ace, there is only one test to find out whether your mission on earth is complete: If you're alive, it isn't! And there is only one fact in life which is absolutely certain: Everything will change in order to remain the same."

We walked in silence while I tried to make sense of what he had said. I thought he was going to explain himself as usual, but he didn't. Eventually I realized that he was waiting for me, so I queried:

"Teecha, your first comment sounds acceptable but how am I supposed to figure out that things change to stay the same?"

"Isn't it strange that just as you're about to enjoy your achievements, or that just when you're about to give up all hope of reaching a goal, things suddenly change? What was important to you at one stage becomes irrelevant with the challenge of something new, and what was a terrible worry yesterday is of no concern today. If it wasn't like that then all beings may as well be spiritless robots, in which case there could hardly be any reason for life. There is life and no living being is spiritless..."

Teecha was his old self again. He kept walking and talking, waved and gestured with his arms and stopped every now and then to point out something of interest. Whether it was dung beetles on the ground, a stick insect between the grass, or an eagle gliding high above, his eyes didn't miss a thing. I remained next to him and Xi'tau followed closely. It was almost like the first day we had walked, except that the air was pleasant and cool and small puddles of muddy water were the only telltales left by the storm.

"You all have your ups and downs while you shape yourselves to life's harmony and the perfect balance of the universe. However, it certainly isn't a good feeling when things do not go your way, when you feel depressed, confused or when you've come to your wits' end. Well, Ace, as you're alive and also changing, let's see why you burden yourself with all kinds of unnecessary worries and what you could do about your own mission.

"First of all you must accept that you are full of inhibitions, phobias, memories of bad experiences, guilt and other negative things. Many of those memories come from your past lives, as memory is something that goes with the spirit and not with your brain…"

All of a sudden a *Namaqua* dove fluttered in front of us with a broken wing. My immediate reaction was to feel sorry for the little bird and I chased after it. I may have been able to mend its wing if I could catch it and release it afterwards. The closer I got to it the more cleverly it dodged me, while the broken wing seemed to heal by itself until the bird flew away strongly, leaving me panting for breath. Confused, I turned to look where Teecha was. He was at least 50 meters back, laughing and pointing to a small shrub next to him. "Come here Ace!" he shouted.

When I reached him he was still smiling and said: "Looks like even Homo sapiens fall for it." He carefully opened some leaves to show a small flimsy nest between the branches. Lying inside it were two chicks about three weeks old. They kept completely still and played dead. With black-specked dull brown feathers I could hardly see them and was dumbfounded, to say the least. The little dove had cleverly distracted me from his nest, but had underestimated Teecha. By then the dove had flown back to us and acted pathetically, drawing its broken wing on the ground a few meters away.

"Let's move on Ace, she's stressing."

A few meters further I had to ask: "Teecha, how is it possible for that bird to be so clever? Who taught it to act like that?"

"Why don't you ask N!odima?" was his answer. When he continued talking I knew the Namaqua incident was closed.

"Most religions believe and base their teachings on the hereafter, or 'life after death'. What then Ace, is so difficult to accept about 'life before life'? If you believe in the hereafter, no matter how a particular religion pictures that in their scripts and teachings, you believe in the immortality of the spirit.

"This is one example from The Bible, Matthew 10 verse 28:

'Do not be afraid of those who kill the body but cannot kill the soul...'

"Eternity is patient: You can have as many tries at life as you want because time will not run out for you. Eternity doesn't care about time. While you are in the school of life, you may have to write out what life means 50 or a 100 times on the blackboard. Life's teachers, probably a few of them, will not let you pass the subject until you understand it. Eheh, Ace, you get many chances at life, not only one. Remember that you have the choice between good and evil, for which you will be held accountable. Recent psychological evidence suggests exactly that, but it is quite different from the 'judgment day' depicted by religious dogma. If a poor and sinful soul will be judged solely by his doings in life on earth, certainly he himself must have access to his own files to defend himself in a court of heaven.

"Memory is the director in charge of your life's movie and your spirit has direct access to it whenever needed. Sometimes, however, memory of certain things is not needed and is best forgotten. How many times does an insignificant incident trigger off some bad experiences in your life, enough to change your mood instantly? Some of those incidents are so insignificant that you're not even consciously aware of them, yet they set off a chain of suggestions and emotions from the subjective mind to the conscious, and you're not always sure of what actually hit you.

"Your good memories are always there, yet instead of making an issue of them, you do so with the bad ones, and worse, you allow those to control your life and your future. You end up with an 'ISI' – an Inadequate Self Image, directing your life..."

"Why is that?"

He stopped, cupped his ear and said: "Listen..."

I listened but heard nothing. "What for?"

"Shhh ...." Far off I heard deep booming sounds like distant drums.

"What's that?"

"The *Lekhotutu* – come, we'll find them."

"Who're they?"

Teecha set off in a new direction and decided to answer my first question instead. "Your conscious or creative mind relies on information received from the subjective mind, which in turn relies on information from all your other minds and senses, including your memory. And, very important Ace, your subjective mind accepts all the information from the creative mind *including imagination*, as the truth. Some of your senses are centered in your body, like the five senses you all know about. Many others, because you were led to believe they're supernatural, are defined as Extra Sensory Perception (ESP) or by other fancy names. A good example is intuition, which you, typical of all males, usually ignore. You shouldn't do that, for it's your gift of knowing in advance."

He stopped and listened but I didn't hear a sound. Then, as we walked on I also heard the ceremonial drums and became a little concerned about what kind of ritual the Lekhotutu were performing.

Teecha wasn't worried.

"Why can't you accept the fact that you all have these other senses and stop thinking of them as supernatural or 'black magic'? There is nothing supernatural about anything, Ace. White magic is as powerful as black magic, and the same ingredients or powers are used for a 'witches brew' as those for the 'bread of life'. It all depends on what you want to use those powers for. In fact, everything is as natural as it was in the past and will be forever. This Inadequate Self Image affects all of you to a greater or lesser degree. It is the one thing that inhibits your potential to such an extent that the average human being uses only a small percentage of his real *'I'*-Power."

"OK, that may be true, but for the second time, why? And the

Lekhotutu, Teecha – are they friendly people?"

"In early childhood you were conditioned to believe that you were no good at performing even trivial tasks. This has a dramatic subconscious influence in your adult life. Furthermore, you were taught loads of nonsense, which you willingly accepted from tutors and other people whom you often hero-worshipped. Here's something to think about:

Young Mary age five sees her mother busy in the house, sweeping the floor and washing up the dishes. Loving her mother dearly she wants to help. Mary takes a broom from the kitchen and starts sweeping the floor. The broom is about three times her size, and very clumsily she tries her best, thinking only about the praise she'll get from Mommy. Mary is ignorant to the fact that Mommy is extremely upset. Daddy invited his colleagues for lunch. It's 11am and the dishwasher has packed up. She hasn't even started to prepare lunch. The inevitable happens – Mary knocks Mommy's precious vase off a shelf in the TV room and it shatters... Can you imagine what follows?

"Johnny of three years old sees Daddy rather busy under the bonnet of the family car, tinkering away and talking to himself in words Johnny has never heard. He feels compelled to help and picks up a monkey-wrench. If Dad tinkers and works so hard, he has to help him. Dad is cursing away at a nut he cannot loosen and he has knocked the skin off his knuckles a few times. Johnny starts to tinker a few dents into the mudguard with a monkey-wrench he can hardly pick up, confident that Dad will be grateful. Dad hears the tinkering and wonders what this new noise in the car's engine is. Puzzled, he looks up. Want to imagine some more?"

The scenes in my mind were upsetting and Teecha knew that: "Eheh, Ace, you're quite right – probably physical punishment after the scream which already frightened the child half to death. 'You stupid little fool, what the hell do you think you're doing!?...' And there goes the child's confidence in his ability to be something. Similar things happen many more times in those early years but children are not easily discouraged. They are also quick to forgive and forget.

"There comes a time though when the words 'You stupid...' 'You clumsy...' 'You useless...' and many others spoken in anger or ignorance, become too much. Too much for the child, so he or she becomes all those negative things, and parents and teachers find it so difficult to understand why Johnny cannot cope with his schooling, why he shows so little interest or why Mary is so rebellious. Poor parents, and they did everything in their lives 'just for them'. What a shame. To make things worse, Johnny and Mary have each lived a couple of lives before, some successful and some maybe not, and their own little ones are now three and five years old respectively.

"Memory stays with the spirit and although some ancient scriptures state that before each new life, man has to drink from 'the river of forgetfulness', the subconscious remembers. According to the Tibetan Book of the Dead, 'between-life' phases exist for each spirit, where it is judged according to its actions and doings in the previous life. This has been verified by thousands of people under hypnotic regression, all of whom described the judgment in a similar way. Apparently it is usual to be judged by three beings of higher existence. The spirit itself and those beings, as well as a guide who is often mentioned, had no bodily form but existed spiritually. The 'judges' were never derogatory. Instead, they were helpful in analyzing where things went wrong and in suggesting what spiritual evolvement should be sought for in the next life.

"The beings knew exactly what had happened in the spirit's previous life and always suggested the right choice for the next one, to undo the wrongs of a former physical existence or to go for a completely new experience. If the spirit was a heartless tyrant in a previous life, its next life experience may be solely for the purpose of protecting the poor and helpless. If it was an arrogant and rich fool, its new life may be spent as a blind beggar in the gutters. The 'what' and 'how' is suggested but not enforced – it is left for the spirit itself to decide. After the judgment the spirit knows what is best and in most cases follow the suggestions of the 'trinity', even if it means that its next life could be spent in utter misery.

"Certain experiences must be gained before there is a chance to move to higher levels of existence.

"Of interest Ace, is the postulation that the idea of a triunal God comes from this deeper knowledge of man, most of you having been through the 'judgment of three' a number of times. It is also strangely consistent with the Kabbalah, the inner teachings of Jewish mysticism. Most people though, who described this between-life existence and judgment, denied the suggestion that the three judges were anything like God. They experienced in that metaconscious state, the presence and existence of the Ultimate Spirit as everything that really matters, the knowledge of all being and truth and the feeling of an all encompassing love. Those who had felt that presence had extreme difficulty describing it in words. It had nothing to do with an Old Testament type God who could be pleased by blood and burnt offerings on an altar."

I stopped and said: "Teecha, I still don't know who you are, but now you're clawing at my soul – I don't think I can handle all of this or even if I want to know anything more. I think we should leave it at that."

"Ace, you came to me – it was not the other way around. You are the one with the questions and you have the choice to believe and to accept whatever you want. Are the things I'm telling you too contradictory to your deep and inner beliefs? I don't think so but if you want to stay in the dark that's your decision."

Those eerie booming drums were closer and I had visions of being led straight into a Lekhotutu witchcraft ceremony as an offering to the devil. I tried to console myself: "Nonsense Uys, in this day and age it cannot be – you're imagining things."

The Bushman waited for me to make a move. "You know he's OK," something told me, and for the first time in many years I listened to intuition: "Teecha, let's find the Lekhotutu."

"I see you've made up your mind. Now, to open it consider this: Most religions give you a man-made god, who likes to sit on a throne, with all his subordinates kneeling down, trembling with fear, singing 'Praise to the Lord' and 'Hallelujah' throughout eternity. This earthly god likes rituals of all kinds, including blood and muck and moo, giving you wine that turns into blood, bread that turns into flesh, telling you constantly how useless and sinful you are, and unless you repent he will smite you into burning hell! However, if you could wash yourself in the blood of Jesus to become 'clean' you may just make it to heaven. How metaphorical is that to Johnny and Mary when they are six years old, Ace?

I was taken by surprise and he continued unchallenged:

"That's the kind of stuff nightmares consist of and their parents wonder why the kids are so scared of the dark. What else do they expect if that same morning in Sunday-school their little ones were taught that they may 'be thrown outside, into the darkness, where there will be weeping and gnashing of teeth'? Could you expect five- or six-year-olds to understand that, or are you adults completely stupid?

"Are your modern rituals any different from those practiced by what you call 'primitive savages'? This earthly god that many of you worship, instructed his followers to wipe out 'man, woman and child', and his holy wars caused and still cause more loss of life, pain and misery on Earth than you care to think about. Is that the straight and narrow road you must follow, splattered with 'heavenly' blood?

"Surely, *the Ultimate Spirit exists on a higher level than that*? Don't you think he expects a bit more from you? "Fearing your man-made god, not seeing the wood for the trees, is another of your conditioned problems. If ever there were going to be false prophets they have already come and gone, and they did a very good job while here.

"Spirits on much higher levels of existence than yourselves came, told you the basic truths, and left. You yourselves and your forefathers chose to twist their words and attach different meanings to them. Then, as more truths are uncovered, like the Dead Sea Scrolls, which were found in a cave on the northwest coast of the Dead Sea in 1947, you scrambled to fit them in with your present beliefs. The contents of some of the scrolls, discovered in various other caves up to the early 1950s, were considered so controversial that it was kept in secrecy for more than 35 years.

"Christianity may have started many years before the birth of Jesus, himself being from a community called the Essenes, who were believed to have written some of the scrolls. An Essene monastery or house of studies, near the Dead Sea, was a major archeological discovery, which became known as the *Qumran* ruins. Jesus may have had his schooling there, as there is a period of about 12 years of his life unaccounted for in the Bible.

"As a matter of interest, the life story of 'Superman' is based on this – Superman too went away for 12 years to learn his powers. The truth, the whole truth and nothing but the truth is elusive.

The following is written in the Qur'an, Sura 4 verses 157-158:

"That they said (in boast),
'We killed Christ Jesus
The son of Mary
The Apostle of God';
But they killed him not,
Nor crucified him, ...
For of a surety
They killed him not:-
Nay, God raised him up
Unto Himself; and God
is Exalted in Power, Wise:'"

"Just something to ponder on Ace, to show how different pasts and cultures cause you to have different beliefs and how easily you are conditioned. Now, having these firmly engraved memories of past experiences, from this life and previous lives, and because you heavily rely on your subjective mind, you live your life mostly on subjective reality, rather than reality itself. Although your conscious mind can easily distinguish between the two, you tend not to believe yourself, let alone to believe others. Instead of calmly and logically analyzing all perceptions you receive or have received a long time ago, and you can do this in a split second, you allow your subjective mind to dictate your actions regarding any situation or emotional experience, based on its own decision on the matter. Rightly so, because you really don't need to concern yourself with its decision, as it will always make the right one, based on all perceived facts available. Perceived facts, because those your subjective mind bases a decision on, may all be imaginary or from ages past and irrelevant to your present or future situation."

Relevant to my present and future situation at the time were the drums of the Lekhotutu, which were getting closer and closer. Teecha had stopped again.

Something was funny though – normally the drums of indigenous tribes sound continuously for hours on end and I'd never heard of the Lekhotutu. Their drums were intermittent, without beat, frightening.

"How far are they, Teecha?"

"Not so far."

Typical of Africa's peoples, 'far' is a concept depending on the situation at hand. 'Not so far' could mean 100 meters or two days' walk. He listened attentively for a few seconds and turned left.

"Eheh," I mimicked – knowing exactly how far they were.

"On the other hand Ace, you can fully control what you want to know or need to know from your subjective mind, once you understand how it functions and once you share your desires with it. You, your conscious mind, have full control over the subjective but if you're mentally lazy, the subjective takes over.

"When you and your subordinates leave the Pheon's control panel, the 'Auto Pilot' assumes control. It will react to stimuli based on its own decisions, depending how well the survival programs were written and tested in the first place.

"This is a fantastic ability of your mind, as the subjective may well save the whole organism should the conscious be otherwise occupied, for example when sleeping, daydreaming or even if the body is completely drugged. A common case which you've personally experienced Ace, is when somebody overindulges in alcohol. Instead of passing out completely (which is usually the case), he continues to be seemingly wide-awake, joking and carrying on as normal. He may even decide to drive his car home, and few of his friends will realize that his conscious mind has long since decided to opt out.

"The person may miraculously make it home, only to wake up the next afternoon looking for aspirins and completely confused – his conscious mind stubbornly refuses to recall any of his actions during his drunken stupor, leaving a couple of hours of his life as a complete blank in memory. Often, during that spiritually unconscious period, the person's true character comes to the fore – as it is known by the subconscious and subjective minds. Be careful unless you want to part with all your secrets.

"In cases like that the subjective takes full control, but it has those major drawbacks of differentiating and distinguishing between time, entities and reality. It is designed to take full control whenever the conscious mind is not in the driver's seat and to act drastically to prevent any situation that may cause undesired spiritual or bodily experiences. Rightly so, but depending on what it has been conditioned to do, by your own self or others, it can control your actions to such an extent that it becomes detrimental to the whole organism: 'You need that drink', 'You must have that fix' or 'You're wasting your time on something impossible', are good examples of how your subjective mind controls the *'I'*.

"You confine and limit yourself to bad experiences and memories, just because you have a problem forgiving yourself and others, or admitting or accepting that you had made a mistake. You are not prepared to forget certain experiences or to re-evaluate beliefs which constantly cloud your vision. In many situations your creative mind says 'Yes!' but your subjective says 'No!' or vice versa. Can you imagine the arguments within yourself, the inner conflict? How destructive is that? No wonder you get ulcers, have migraine attacks, drive yourselves to alcohol or drugs, give up everything, get the 'yuppie flu', become terminally ill with cancer and even commit suicide. Very, very negative, but true."

"Hang on Teecha! Are you telling me that all those things are the result of my attitude towards life? How can I help it if I feel a certain way about things – I have my own principles, you know!"

"You hang on Ace, and don't get so uptight about it! A lot of what your subjective mind has available as reality or truth, was not engraved there yourself: You are full of brainwashed beliefs telling you that you're useless and delivered in sin and that to levitate is impossible. Those same beliefs prevent you from moving objects with your mind. What do you think lifted your 4x4 out of the ant bear hole? Your word for that is 'psychokinesis,' meaning 'to move objects by mental influence without physical contact'. You have the fancy word but no knowledge of how or why it works. There are many cases where children, 'not knowing better', performed impossible feats. Impossible you say, because you think it impossible. Who made you think so in the first place, and why is it impossible? Your best answer to that will probably be: 'They told me so...' Who are 'They' Ace? No wonder that most kids as they grow older, start believing that whatever they could do or want to do is impossible, and therefore lose the ability or interest to do it."

The drums sounded again, 'not so far'. Teecha held up his hand and looked around. Doing the same I saw nothing, even when standing on my toes. Bent slightly forward, he walked on cautiously. "Time to walk behind yourself," he said.

I assumed the same posture and followed. Boom... boom… This time I got a little nervous and whispered: "Who are these people, Teecha?" He didn't hear me.

"To come back to your perception of reality: the next time you have to make a decision, your mind takes real reality, imagined reality and associated memories from ages past into account and Bang! – ambivalent emotions, unexpected conflict and big problems. Possible outcome: a terrible headache, and not necessarily through your own doing. Furthermore, if you had said or even thought that 'stupid fool' bit about somebody else (there are these things called ESP), you may well have to go to the chemist to buy him or her some headache pills. Worse, you have all been so 'spiritwashed' since childhood and long before, by society, religion, parents, tutors and what have you, that it is almost impossible to rely on your clever subjective mind – it is cluttered with garbage. When the crunch comes, your creative mind relies on this garbage, with a predictable outcome, called 'GIGO' by computer programmers: 'Garbage In, Garbage Out!' Yet daily you continue to push those powerful little buttons."

Once again something intuitive told me he was right as he cautiously zigzagged between shrubs to make use of every bit of cover. He didn't seem to worry about talking though.

"Won't they hear us?" I whispered.

"*Aowa*, they have other things on their mind."

"Teecha, what you said just now is dangerous stuff. What can I do about it? How can I straighten the mess out?"

"Only by understanding why you react strangely under certain circumstances, why you can't stand this or that, why you are scared of heights or spiders, why you like or dislike a particular person, why, why, why. OK, so obviously the first question to ask yourself is: why? Why do I think it's impossible? Why do I get angry when someone makes a trivial mistake? Why do I shout or scream at someone? Why am I unhappy? Why am I always sick? Why do I believe this or that? Of course, you may not get all the answers straightaway, but continue with your self-analysis: Did this or that really happen to me? Is this fact that I firmly believe in really the truth? Am I really scared of something as harmless as frogs? Can I really never be happy? Can I not forgive and forget this or that incident about myself or somebody else? Does it matter?

"Self-analysis may take you a very long time with constant and continuous effort because you all have many skeletons in the closet. You also have many worn out beliefs, deviations, detours, 'no entry' and 'keep out' signs in your memory banks, so much so that you do not even allow yourself a glimpse of what may be seen.

"Yet all the time, you rely on this fantastic computer, your mind, to come up with the right answers to all your problems. Isn't it a little unrealistic and unfair Ace? Eheh, unfair to yourself and to those close to you. Unfair to the Ultimate Spirit of which you are a part. Unfair to all other spirits, especially to those who look up to you for direction, like your children. Did you really have to spirit-wash them too with 'original sin', when there is 'original innocence' and 'original love', all the way from eternity?"

I wanted to say something but couldn't – the words didn't form.

"Eheh – true Ace, you have to help them along because it's one of your missions in life – to show them the right way as far as possible. You have to tell them what is good and bad, although they'll make up their own minds about that sooner than you think. You can advise them what to search for in life and what to watch out for in life. You should make them aware of the beauty and the ugliness of life, and you should teach them what the balance is all about. You must show them life.

"What you do not have to tell them is that they are 'delivered in sin', no good at all, that they have to be forgiven and that they must 'repent' before they can go to heaven and all that absolute bullshit. What sins? Your own? Now think seriously about what you're all doing. An innocent baby child is the greatest and most cherished gift of love that God gives to any parent, and then while baptizing it, most of you solemnly promise in very similar words: 'Thank you ever so much dear God, I'll try my best to take care of and to teach this sinfully received little brat the secrets of your kingdom'. Does that make any sense Ace, especially after a Great Spirit had told you this:

'Let the children come to me, and do not hinder them, for the kingdom of God belongs to such as those.'

"You know who spoke those words so why don't you tell your

children how fantastic they are, what powers they have, how they could and should use them and that their potential is unlimited? Are you scared to, lest they end up showing you the way? You probably all are, for parents, teachers, society and religions alike, do their utmost to tell toddlers and kids that they are nothing, useless, and full of sin. And, as you will see more of what your mind can do, most of them believe exactly that, and you end up with a 'sick' society: '*The sins of the fathers will be visited upon the children...*'"

Teecha was almost shouting and I was sure that the Lekhotutu must have heard us, for the drums were quiet. My head was spinning and the sun beetles helped it along. I felt exactly like many years ago after a good scolding, but this time I had the courage to ask:

"OK... Now what? How do I get myself back on the track? How do I rid myself of my hang-ups and where do I find help?"

"There are many options Ace. I mentioned self-analysis and asking yourself 'why?' You can look to parents, friends and spouses for help. You can go to psychologists, psychiatrists, spiritualists, marriage counselors and the like. You can be converted to one of the 20,000 different religions, sects and cults on Earth, and you can allow yourself to be hypnotized, letting somebody else loose in your mind. There is nothing wrong with any of these options – you all need other people to help you along and in some cases you need professional help. Most people are sincere in their efforts to help and from time to time you all need a shoulder to cry on.

"Beware of sympathy though – it kills! To give someone sympathy is to keep him right down in the mud instead of helping him out. If this is difficult to fathom, then consider the fact that 'Not only does misery love company, it loves other miserable company!' Rather have empathy with someone, which means that you could have a deep and sincere understanding of his problems but that you can help him to do something positive about them. When you need help, you need someone who can help you to help yourself for that is what you're all looking for – how to help yourself. The saying goes: 'God helps those who help themselves'.

If you do not have the desire to help yourself, then there is nothing more to say.

"Anyway, you are all able to clear your minds of rubbish, to start with a clean slate, to demolish the barriers you built in your lives or allowed to be built and to use your unlimited potential. It is quite easy...

"Just as the subjective mind has the power to destroy you if allowed to, so it has the power to enable you to be everything you want and to have everything you want, if allowed. Fortunately, you yourself are in control of your conscious mind because you are it, you are the spirit.

"Nothing could ever go wrong with your spirit – it cannot even die. The only problem a spirit may have is that its 'vehicle' or some of its minds may malfunction, generally with its own consent. Eheh, with its own consent because you can command your mind and body to do whatever you want. You have been told how this works in many different scriptures – Luke 11 verse 9 is one example:

'Ask and it will be given to you; seek and you will find, knock and the door will be opened to you. For everyone who asks receives; he who seeks finds and to him who knocks, the door will be opened.'

"It is so true Ace – tell your mind what to do and it does it. Tell it what to look for and it finds it. Tell it to solve a problem, taking imagined reality into account and it computes the answer. Tell it to get rid of the garbage in your memory banks and it will do so. Tell it you want to be happy and it finds a way. Tell it you want to be healthy and you are. Better still, imagine you are happy and it keeps you happy, imagine you are healthy and you stay healthy. Tell it what you are in life and imagine what you will be in life and it will make all the plans to make you what you think you are and what you can become. It will do so either in a negative or in a positive way – the choice is yours and yours alone. I must stress this point Ace – you are what you think you are, and you become whatever you imagine yourself to be. Your creative conscious mind is in control, and whatever it decides, whatever goal it wants to reach, everything else will fall in line."

Teecha grabbed me by the shoulder and pushed me down, so that we both ended up on our haunches.

"What now?"

"Shhh ... It's the Lekhotutu – they're straight ahead. Stay down and follow me."

As he crawled ahead, there came a loud 'Boom! boom! boom!' from in front. The drums couldn't have been more than 50 meters away and my heart's pace increased considerably. I crawled on hands and knees after Teecha. He paused every three to four meters to peep over the top of the tall grass. A sound from behind and my heart stopped. Turning around slowly, I expected to look up the pointing assegais of staring Lekhotutu warriors. It was only a stalking lion and I sighed with relief. Xi'tau was behind me all the time and decided to join the action. I turned forward and crawled on.

Teecha stopped and beckoned me towards him. He parted the grass and leaves, opened his hand forward in a gesture for me to look and said: "The Lekhotutu ..."

There was a large patch of burnt grass in front of us, probably set alight by the lightning that morning. Xi'tau also wanted to look and brushed past me but Teecha pushed his head aside. Less than 20 meters from us were two big black birds, the size of turkeys. They had long thick black beaks and the male was showing off. The red air sack underneath his throat was puffed up and he dragged his opened wings on the ground. 'Boom!... boom!... boom... boom!'

"Teecha, that's ground hornbills!" I exclaimed softly. "You so-and-so – you said they were people!"

"*Aowa*, Ace, I never said so – you imagined that as soon as you heard them, so I left you to it. *Tchi... tchi...* Savages with bones through their noses? Witchcraft and evil rituals?"

He burst out laughing. As he did so the birds took flight and they transformed from awkwardly comical to beautiful winged creatures of red, white and black. I smiled at first and then laughed louder than Teecha did. The birds flew a wide circle over our heads and landed just a little further away, still in the burnt patch.

Unconcerned about us, they continued their courting and booming. From where we stood, it looked rather more like an argument between the two.

"Do you know what they're saying Ace?"

"No idea."

"She is saying: I'm going, I'm going – I'm going home to my family, and he is saying; You can go… You can go… You can go if you want!"

I laughed some more.

We turned back to camp. I started to accept Teecha's doctrine about imagination. To tell the truth, I was actually disappointed to find that my Lekhotutu warriors were birds, but they proved a point: Imagination is a powerful thing. Something else worried me though. I could imagine myself successful and happy and to do all the things I dreamt about, but where would I find the money? How could I do those things without money? I wished I were a Bushman for they have no use for money, unlike me in the big city, where survival and happiness depended on how much you have of it. Then I questioned that belief, for a few months ago I was amongst the *Ovahimba* tribe in a remote part of North-West Namibia. The Himba's had no use for money – they refused to accept it in exchange for anything because to them it was worthless. They couldn't buy anything with money because there were no roads, no shops, no villages, nothing 'civilized' in their land. Yet they were happy, contented and beautiful – the last nomads of Africa.

Teecha was eavesdropping my thoughts:

"Ace, that's another truth of life: You will always have more than enough money to do what you want to do. Money is directly proportional to what you want to be and what you want to do with your mission on Earth. It doesn't work the other way around – your desires and ambitions are never proportional to what you want to or can do with money. It is said that you are all equal, some of you just more equal than others. To be more equal requires a little more effort. There is nothing wrong with having more in life, expecting more from life and being more in life. One serious sin though is to sit on your behind and to do nothing, waiting for things to happen and complaining bitterly that nothing happens your way.

There are three kinds of spirits:

Those who make things happen,

Those who watch what happens and

Those who wonder what happened.

"Another sin is to wish your life away. There is no such thing as 'I wish I had the money' or 'I wish I could do this or that' or 'I wish I had a better job.' Wishing does not work – it is the direct opposite to positive imagination, which leads to a clear knowledge of what you want in life, which in turn becomes reality. A wish is a thought in the wind.

"Once you know what you want, what you want to achieve and why you want to achieve it, you can embark on any of a number of different journeys to reach your goals. More than enough money will appear en route but not at the start of the journey, as it is the least important thing. If there is no goal, no idea, no dream to follow, then what do you need money for? To survive? What do you want to survive for if you have no reason for living?

"Ace, think about the fact that there is more to any journey or adventure than merely to arrive at your destiny. For you the journey to a destiny where you have never been is the adventure in itself. You haven't reached your ultimate destiny yet, so why don't you relax and enjoy the trip, why don't you turn it into a fantastic adventure? If the only purpose of your life was to enjoy your annual three-week holiday, getting to your destination as fast as possible, then life, like the holiday, may just be over too soon. If you have a destiny to reach, a purpose, something to discover, a dream, then the excitement and adventure of traveling through the jungle of life, to find a way, to see and experience the as yet unknown, becomes a challenge and something to enjoy. And I must stress this too – there will always be more than enough money along the way.

"A word of caution though – don't start a journey where you know the end is a 'cul de sac', when you know you're not ready for it, or when you know it will not be to the benefit of yourself and all other spirits. Use your intuition and do not go against it. Eheh, you know what the future holds because your desires and imaginations become reality – *you control your own destiny*. It is as simple as that. Imagine your cup of tea, then go make it.

"Unfortunately Ace, the opposite is also true. Tell your mind that you do not want to go anywhere, and you stay where you are. Tell it you are tired of life, and you'll have no energy to live. Tell it you are sick, and if you're lucky you'll only catch a cold. Tell it you are of no use to anybody, and forget about a career. Tell it nobody loves you, and you get sympathy. Think you are old, and your body believes you. Tell yourself that you'll never have the money and whatever you may have, will be taken away. Tell your child that he or she is stupid and will never be anything in life and you've planted the weeds and watered them well.

"It's an incredibly powerful thing, the mind. Something you really have to learn to control or else it could destroy you. On the other hand it could take you beyond the limits of imagination. Do you remember that I said the top of the pyramid of needs was only the beginning?"

"Yes – Why?"

"Just about every religion on earth, every culture, first world nation and many 'primitive' tribes (he showed the quotes with his fingers), have this idea that persons must be 'initiated' into a society, a religion, culture or tribe. This always takes place with a ceremony of some kind, like a 21st birthday with a silver or gold 'key to the door of life', the barmitzvah (a religious initiation for 13 year old Jewish boys), a tribal initiation school and rituals, baptizing, religious rebirth, acceptance as a Freemason and the like. All of these say the same thing: that after the ceremony those persons are OK, only then can they be accepted into society, the movement or culture. Only then do they 'know'."

"Yes, I've been through some of those – for what they're worth," I agreed. "They taught me little if anything about life. I'd like to know more and to reach my real potential in life."

"There's no ceremony for that, but I'll explain it with the pyramid of needs. Each of the stages, from physiological needs to esteem and self-actualization, are accompanied by a stage of spiritual development, which could be superimposed over the five stages of needs shown by the pyramid. Spiritual development is the aim and purpose of existence, which happens over many lifetimes and during many 'between-life' stages. Corresponding to each of the five basic needs, spiritual development takes place as soul searching and spiritual evolution, also advancing through five stages.

They are:

Materialism – where the biggest concern is for physical well-being and sensual emotions. There is hardly any concern for the feelings of others and no consciousness or interest in an afterlife or spiritual existence.

Superstition – when there is an awareness of other forces and spiritual entities without any knowledge about them, leading to fears, primitive rituals and beliefs in black magic and lucky charms. The desire for material possessions and power is still all-important.

Fundamentalism – leading to the belief in an Almighty God who has to be worshipped through religious dogma and rules. Superstition and rituals prevail but there is a belief in an afterlife or heaven, which will be the reward for good conduct. Fear of the Almighty God leads to the requirement for leaders, high priests and saviors as mediators.

Philosophy – which is an awakening to the self as part of the existence of all. Religious beliefs prevail, but they are questioned as the deeper meanings and teachings of the scriptures are appreciated. This stage shows a respect for life and sincere appreciation for the feelings and beliefs of others.

Questing – the desire to understand the meaning and purpose of life, now knowing that there is an ultimate reason for existence. There is uncertainty and anxiety of how to go about attaining further spiritual growth. This quest often results in extensive study of the metaphysical, investigating or joining various different religions, cults or groups. It may even result in living with the minimum physical necessities in the desert or in a mountain hermitage.

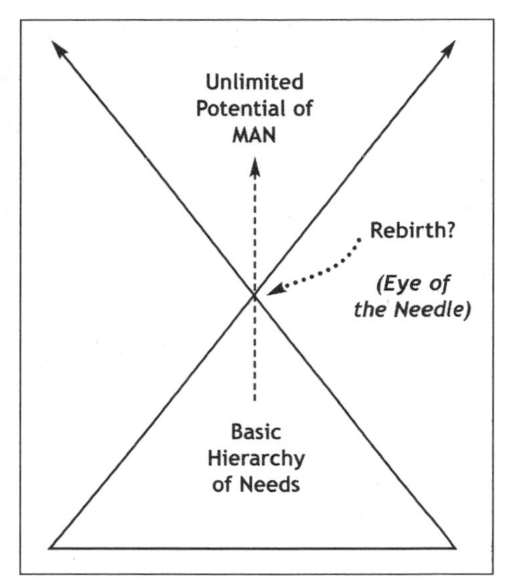

Figure 4: Life Above the Pyramid

"The top level of the pyramid of needs is called 'self actualization'. If you superimpose the five stages of spiritual development over that, 'Questing' is also at the top. Does your potential stop there, Ace?"

"Don't know... No wait, I think I know it doesn't."

Teecha took his digging stick and scratched figure 4 on the ground.

He explained: "Most certainly not, because now the pyramid's sides extends infinitely like this, opening up an unlimited potential with no further boundaries. Once through 'the eye of the needle' there are no more limits, no concern for basic needs but only a realization of the 'Oneness' of life itself, which you could call being 'reborn' if you like. Here is where things happen rather differently to what you're used to...

"*The more you give, the more you receive... The more you help, the more you can hope for... The more you teach the more you learn... The happier you make others, the more you have to enjoy and to laugh about... The more you support others, the more assistance you get... By pulling others along, you are pushed along... The more you respect life, any form of it, the longer and healthier is your own life... The less you worry about money, the more you are guarded against misfortune... The more you see, the more beautiful and perfect life becomes...*

"It is here where imagination becomes reality, Ace. It's like magic but most importantly, it is here where you realize the greatest principle of all: The more you LOVE the more you know your reason for being and the more you become One with Life,

One with the Universe, and One with the Ultimate Spirit..."

THE RETURN

If ever I have experienced ambivalent emotions it was that morning when I had to bid Teecha farewell. I would have liked to stretch my stay another day but it just wasn't possible. I had to get back to Johannesburg and had to phone home. Pushing my luck, there may have been a telephone in the small village called Tshabong, or maybe at the border post at McCarthy's Rest, some 200 miles or 300 kilometers away. Having decided to leave early, I had packed most of the camping equipment the previous night, trying not to disturb Xi'tau, who still thought it was his right to sleep on the roof-carrier.

After filling a Thermos flask with boiling water, I reluctantly packed the remaining few items and checked all the ropes and knots holding the equipment down. Xi'tau must have realized that his bed was going to leave. Lying underneath the big acacia, he watched my activities with little interest. Teecha sat cross-legged under the same tree playing his pipe. It sounded like he was practicing, the tunes intermittent and lonely, sometimes without melody. Having learned that all good experiences eventually end, I finally picked up enough courage and walked over to them.

"Teecha, I can't express my feelings but by now you know that I know that you already know them. Anyway, I must go."

He put the Se!warra'warra into his bag, stood up smiling and said:

"Eheh, you have your destiny and I have mine, but before we part I have a few more things to tell you."

"I'd love to stay longer but..."

"Don't be so concerned about time, Ace!

We probably won't meet again for eons to come, and wouldn't you like to know what your journey really means?"

Suddenly I realized that he wasn't referring to my destiny for that particular day, so for the moment curiosity won again: "Five minutes Teecha – the sun isn't patient."

"Ace, there is more to any journey than just transporting yourself from point A to B. However, the journey through life to Destiny is the one where the fact of arriving could be the ultimate experience. But once we reach that destiny, wherever and whenever in eternity, we will be left with one more limit to cross."

"My goodness Teecha, I thought that once we achieve that we'd have nothing else to worry about." I smiled but then cynically asked him: "So what could that limit be? By then we'll all be gods!"

He showed no emotion and replied:

"We have all set sail to Destiny on board the ship of the mind. This will take you on many adventures and you may decide to change course many times. You know that you cannot take anything along except experience, wisdom and faith, and you know that you have a choice. You know that your minds and the Ultimate Spirit are the most powerful things you'll ever encounter, so learn to use your minds and to make things happen. To do this, you must know who you are and imagine what you will be in the future, which is right now in the present. In other words you must get a clear picture in your minds' eye of yourself, what you are already achieving and what your relationship with everybody and everything around you 'already' is."

I was getting impatient and wanted to get on the road but managed to control myself. "Yes, you've told me that before," I commented, while taking the opportunity test more knots. Teecha was unperturbed by my haste:

"The Universe has an eternal balance. Every spirit has a 'twin soul' or 'soul mate', one the opposite of the other. So opposite that one could be classified as male and the other female. We all need a companion on our journey to Destiny and if we find the right one, our trip will be filled with enrichment such as we can hardly imagine. Many of us have already found our twin soul, yet, being so different in many ways, it is difficult to 'spiritually' find one another. We have built so many walls around ourselves that nobody can really reach us. This 'oppositeness' which attracted us to our soul mate in the first place, can easily destroy what could have been a fantastic relationship.

"We all need to understand this very clearly Ace, and realize that if we choose to ignore it we could end up very lonely. If however, we accept the fact that another spirit can make us 'whole', our powers to face any obstacle, to reach any goal and to enjoy life's journey to the fullest are unlimited. Even the Ultimate Spirit, perceived by most to be masculine, has a feminine Twin Spirit. She is referred to as '*Wisdom*' in many of your ancient scripts including The Bible. Take note of this:

'For at the gates of the Mighty, She hath
taken a seat, and at the entrance thereof
chanteth her song:
In the beginning, before the Lord made the Earth
When He furnished the Heavens, I was with Him;
*and when He set apart His throne on the wind*s
When He set to the sea its bound,
and the waters passed not the word of His mouth
I was harmonizing with Him. I was the one in whom
He delighted, and I was daily gladdened by His presence
on all occasions.'

"What you should think about Ace, is that 'We'-power is infinitely more powerful than 'I'-power."

Teecha certainly had a way to mix me up. I listened without saying a word to what I knew was the last bit of knowledge he was going to share:

"We all have the desire to create. We invent useful tools and machinery. We harness the forces of the universe. We learn about and experience the meaning of life.

We create beautiful art, poetry and music. We build magnificent buildings, conceive fantastic ideas and form lasting relationships, and we're starting to understand the principles of life and love. We're on this journey to learn and to understand much more, to be much more, to pick the fruit from the middle of the garden, to be like the Ultimate Spirit, to become One with It, to be the Whole, the Balance, Life itself.

"However, even should we manage to create a galaxy of stars along our journey, it would be like chasing the wind, meaningless, until through spiritual love: *We conceive something like a real flower, leaving imagination as the only limit*."

Teecha gave me his hand. "*Sepela gabotse*, Ace," he said, which means: 'Go well' in the Sotho language. This time he held my hand even longer than when we had first met. I felt tears rising, swallowed twice and finally managed to say: "Thank you Teecha," before letting go of his hand. I didn't know what to do next so I removed the sheath knife from my belt and handed it to him. "Here, its yours. And by the way, you still haven't told me where all the spirits come from, you know."

He accepted the knife and looked very pleased. In return he held out one of his spears and said: "Here, it's yours. And I see that you now understand your own destiny."

Taking his spear, I purposefully walked to the Landcruiser, but before opening the door turned round and faced him again. He stood watching me silently. For the second time since we had met I saw tears in his eyes. I was still undecided on his origin but at the same time truly amazed with the Bushman. Xi'tau got up and slowly walked towards me. "You're not saying good-bye to him?" Teecha asked.

The lion walked straight up to me and sat down, staring me in the face. Slowly, as if compelled by an unknown force, I held out my opened hand. Xi'tau licked my fingers once and then turned his big head, gesturing that he wanted me to pat him. Having done that, he held up his left forepaw. I took it with both hands and only then realized the size of it. Noticing a tick between his toes, I had trouble removing it, as I couldn't see properly. There was nothing else to do so I said once again: "Thank you..."

Letting go of his paw I climbed into the vehicle. Xi'tau kept staring at me, as if he couldn't understand why I was going to leave. No way can I describe the mixture of emotions I felt. I shoved Teecha's spear behind the seat.

Starting up, I wanted to ask him one last question. Lowering the window, I called: “Teecha, tell me your real name, please!”

“Around here they call me ‘*Morutisi*’,” he shouted. While I shifted the gears into low range and 4-wheel drive, he tied the knife onto his waist, picked up his skin-bag and remaining spear and turned for the bush. Xi’tau followed him as I pulled away.

Morutisi means ‘The Teacher’.

A hundred or so meters further I stopped on top of a small sand ridge. Unsure whether I was dreaming, I looked back. A small frail Bushman with shining white hair and an enormous Kalahari lion next to him, stood in the now empty campsite looking back at me. I waved through the window. Teecha waved back with only one spear held high above his head. I searched for a cigarette, lit it and looked back. Teecha was gone but the lion still stood there, staring at me. Then he started to roar. It was the same roar I had heard that afternoon before meeting Teecha. My skin turned gooseflesh but I found some reality in the vehicle’s accelerator pedal.

Not ten minutes later I came across a herd of wildebeest. At first some of them ran away but then stopped and calmly started to browse again. I drove slowly through them as they were all over the road, like cattle. It was strange. Going around another bend, a big and ugly wildebeest stood in the middle of the road. It was Scar-face’s herd. He looked straight at me with one good eye, shook his head and then moved out of the way. As I passed him, I couldn’t help but shout:

“So you stayed, old fellow – good decision!”

Driving on, I was lost in thought for more than an hour. The road was fair and firm as the rain from the previous day had settled the sand and dust. Only when it returned to its familiar dusty self did I become aware of my surroundings again. True to form, the rain had fallen in a strip of only a few kilometers – a mile or two – wide, as the storm abated itself on a path decided by the elements. The rest of the Kalahari was dry and hot.

Wondering what day it was, I removed my watch from the glove compartment. Without putting it on, I looked at the digital display, which showed that it was 10:22 am.

"Should have left earlier," I told myself. Pushing some buttons on the watch's side, it showed me the date, in typical American format: '4:16 WE'. Driving with one hand, I shook the electronic watch and put it to my ear as if I should hear it ticking. Looking at the LCD display again I decided that the battery must be flat.

"No, can't be – these batteries last for five years or more, and I only bought the watch a few months ago."

Stopping, I checked all its buttons and features. The stopwatch worked and the alarm sounded when tested. Everything was fine except for the date. It stubbornly showed Wednesday 16 April.

"Impossible," I mumbled as my mind started to race. I had never adjusted it and I had spent at least six or seven days with Teecha.

"Cheap stuff," I decided – "it must at least be Sunday the 20th or Monday the 21st."

Concerned, I rummaged through my document folder looking for the itinerary of the clients I had taken on the Namibian safari. Sure enough, I dropped them off at the airport near Windhoek, the Namibian capital, on Monday 14 April for their return flight to Rome. That was more than a week ago. Not knowing what to believe, I switched on the radio. Having no success with FM or medium wave, I switched it to short-wave and tuned into an audible channel. It picked up Radio Botswana with the usual short-wave interferences. As the music died away, I clearly heard a woman announcer:

"This is Radio Botswana. It is now ten-thirty on a clear Wednesday, the sixteenth of April. In the news today..."

The rest I didn't hear. Staring at the dents and scratches on the Landcruiser's bonnet I fumbled with both hands around my waist for my knife. It wasn't there. Then I slowly reached behind the seat and felt

Teecha's spear. The Kalahari started spinning and my body shook like a leaf. Struggling to find first gear, I jerked the clutch and the 4x4 shot forward. To stop my shaking leg from slipping off the accelerator, I pushed my knee down with one hand and tried driving with the other.

For the rest of that journey I had only one destiny in mind:

'Home'...

APPENDIX

BOTANICAL & ZOOLOGICAL NAMES

Common Name	**Scientific Name**	**SA No.** (Trees)
Ant bear / Aardvark	Orycteropus afer	
Bateleur eagle	Terathopius ecaudatus	
Black backed jackal	Canis mesomelas	
Black korhaan	Eupoditis afra	
Blade thorn	Acacia fleckii	165
Baobab tree	Adansonia digitata	467
Buffalo thorn	Ziziphus mucronata	447
Bush baby	Galago moholi	
Bushmen candles	Acacia hebeclada	170
Comiphora (Kanniedood)	Commiphora africana	270
Camel thorn	Acacia erioloba	168
Donkey berries	Grewia flavescens	459,2
Egrets	Bubulcus ibis	
Eland	Taurotragus oryx	
Euphorbia	Euphorbia species (various)	
Greater honeyguide	Indicator indicator	
Grey loerie	Corythaixoides concolor	
Ground hornbills	Bucorvus leadbeateri	
Ground squirrel	Xerus inauris	
Guinea fowl	Numida meleagris	
Honey badger	Mellivora capensis	
Hook thorn	Acacia mellifera	176
Kudu	Tragelaphus strepsiceros	
Leadwood tree	Combretum imberbe	539
Lion	Panthera leo	

Leopard	Panthera pardus	
Makalani palm	Hyphaene benguellensis	24
(also illala palm)	(similar to sp natalensis)	23
Man	Homo sapiens	
Marula tree	Sclerocarya birrea	360
Monkey orange tree	Strychnos cocculoides	623
Mopane tree	Colophospermum mopane	198
Nightjar	Caprimulgus species (various)	
Oryx (Gemsbok)	Oryx gazella	
Ostrich	Struthio camelus	
Pufadder	Bitis arientans arientans	
Rain tree	Lonchocarpus capassa	238
Resin bush	Ozoroa paniculosa	375
Russet bushwillow	Combretum hereroense	538
Sand camwood	Baphia massaiensis	223
Scops owl	Otus scops	
Sheppard's tree	Boscia albitrunca	122
Sickle bush	Dichrostachys cinerea	190
Spotted hyena	Crocuta crocuta	
Springbok	Antidorcas marsupalis	
Springhare	Pedetes capensis	
Steenbok	Raphicerus campestris	
Swainson's francolin	Pternistis swainsoni	
Sweet thorn	Acacia karoo	172
Umbrella thorn	Acacia tortillis	188
Vaalbos	Terminalia sericea	551
Vultures	Gyps africanus and	
Torgos tracheliotus		
	(most common)	
Wildebeest (Gnu)	Connochaetus taurinus	
Zebra	Equus burchelli